Advance Praise for Silver Bullet Selling

"*Silver Bullet Selling* is as valuable to a sales person as shiny shoes and a good territory. I love the book!"
—Stuart Chant, Regional Manager and Trainer, Rewards Network

"The Silver Bullet process helped us develop relationships, uncover opportunities, and better serve our customers. And the people who we thought would reject the process actually embraced it. Our goal is to blend the Silver Bullet process into our culture."
—Jim Roe, President, Arlington/Roe & Co.

"The Barticks have captured the common sense of selling in a way that will benefit both novices and seasoned pros. I will be implementing their six steps daily, and reviewing this book often."
—Stephen Shaner, Manager, HealthPartners Regional Technology Center, Speaker with Attitude

"G.A. and Paul have created a structured and easy-to-follow relationship-building process that can enhance the bottom line of any organization. Whether you're a trainee or seasoned veteran, implementing these techniques into your practice can boost your performance to new heights."
—Milford L. Stern, President and CEO, M.L. Stern & Co., LLC

"The Silver Bullet process has given me the ammunition I need to bring in new business and grow my accounts. It works whether I'm handling the simplest settlement or the most complicated multiproperty real estate transaction. Apply it daily and watch your business grow!"
—T. Scott Jackson, Account Executive, First American Title

SILVER BULLET SELLING

Six Critical Steps to Opening More Relationships and Closing More Sales

G.A. BARTICK
PAUL BARTICK

WILEY

John Wiley & Sons, Inc.

Published by John Wiley & Sons, Inc., Hoboken, New Jersey.
Published simultaneously in Canada.

For general information on our other products and services or for technical support, please contact our
Customer Care Department within the United States at (800) 762-2974, outside the United States at
(317) 572-3993 or fax (317) 572-4002.

Wiley also publishes its books in a variety of electronic formats. Some content that appears in print
may not be available in electronic books. For more information about Wiley products, visit our web
site at www.wiley.com.

Library of Congress Cataloging-in-Publication Data:

Bartick, G. A.
   Silver bullet selling : six critical steps to opening more relationships
and closing more sales / G.A. Bartick, Paul Bartick.
      p.   cm.
   Includes index.
   ISBN 978-0-470-37300-2 (cloth)
   1. Selling.   I. Bartick, Paul.   II. Title.
   HF5438.25.B367 2008
   658.85–dc22

2008028069

Printed in the United States of America.

10 9 8 7 6 5 4 3 2 1

To my loving and supportive wife, Kelly, and my three wonderful kids, Alicia, Carlyn, and Jack. Being able to come home to all of you makes my time on the road worthwhile.

—G.A.

This book is dedicated with love and laughter to my loving wife, Shelley, and children, Kate and Max. You nourish my soul. Let the fun begin anew.

—Paul

This book is also dedicated to our mother, Alyn, for her love and support and for being our biggest cheerleader and fan.

—G.A./Paul

Contents

Foreword

In early 1997, I called G.A. Bartick and asked him to help me with a sales training project we had sold. OutSell was a fledgling company, and we simply didn't have a team big enough to deliver the hundreds of events we had scheduled. The reason I called G.A. was because he had tremendous enthusiasm, was eager to learn, and had the kind of personality that lit up a room. That was G.A.'s first introduction into the world of sales consulting and training, and he was an out-of-the-park success from day one.

G.A. claims he's not a natural, and I'll admit he had a lot to learn when it came to the nuts and bolts of selling and the processes that enable a successful sale to happen. This book gives you everything G.A. learned on his path to becoming one of the nation's leading experts on sales excellence and what it takes to really make it in the competitive world of selling.

Silver Bullet Selling comes directly from the lessons that G.A. and all of us learned over the years as we studied both successful and unsuccessful sales and customer service organizations. Every day at OutSell, consultants interview and work with successful and not-so-successful salespeople, customer service people, sales managers, and sales executives. Spending all those hours with proven top performers is a powerful learning experience. This book shares the secrets and insights that OutSell has gathered on the road, in the trenches, face-to-face with real live breathing salespeople.

The selling ideas in this book come from this real world, not some academic laboratory. These ideas are not theories or a "marketing concept" to launch a new company. OutSell has been working with clients since 1996, and the book is a treasure trove of all the ideas that have been shared by committed and motivated professionals who want to succeed the right way, with integrity and honesty.

G.A. Bartick is the real deal, my friends. I have known him my entire life. There is no one in the world that I have found who has more integrity and is more honestly committed to the success of others. In this book, G.A. shares the powerful methods he has learned and taught to thousands and thousands of selling professionals all over the world for more than a decade. Anyone in sales who reads this book, applies these techniques, and is committed to excellence will achieve more than they ever thought possible in their sales career.

Michael St. Lawrence
Founder, OutSell Consulting, Inc.
Bestselling author of
If You're Not Out Selling,
You're Being Outsold

Acknowledgments

John F. Kennedy got it right: "As we express our gratitude, we must never forget that the highest appreciation is not to utter words, but to live by them." As we finish the final keystrokes and bring this book to a close, we feel deep gratitude to the people in our lives who do double duty. Not only have they helped us develop this book, but more importantly, they are our role models and inspiration every day.

Our families: Kelly, Alicia, Carlyn and Jack; and Shelley, Max and Kate: You deserve special recognition because you are our rock.

Our brother David, mother Alyn, and father Gary: For the profound influence you've had on our lives and our thinking.

Our extended family, Blaze, Terry, Jackie, Donna, Jack, Sandra, Sharon, Howard, Tom, and Marty: For the support and guidance you continue to give us.

Even though it is G.A.'s voice you will hear throughout the book, understand that the content is a confluence of ideas and talents from a great OutSell team. We are deeply grateful to Michael St. Lawrence, the founder of OutSell and the one who saw the inner salesman that was hiding deep, deep inside G.A. We are also greatly indebted to members of the OutSell team, including Brian Lowery, Kent McDougall, Brian Quinn, Dennis Klemp, Jeff Kirschenmann, Mark Woodland, Chris Peterson, Susan Sullivan, Jack Litzelfelner, and Nate Brooks. These are the brave souls who have been out there with us on the front lines, collecting all of the best practices that went into the Silver Bullet process.

We have been blessed to work with some of the best in the publishing business. Martha Jewett, our literary agent, did much more than represent our book. She worked with us when the book was nothing more than an idea, and she advised us every step of the way. Richard Narramore,

Senior Editor, and Tiffany Groglio, the Editorial Assistant at John Wiley & Sons, turned the text from a manuscript into a book we are very proud of. Darrell Smith, our designer and marketing consultant, works tirelessly on our behalf and created the killer cover design.

Thank you to the thousands of sales professionals who have allowed us to poke, prod, observe, and study them. And thank you to you, the readers of this book. We hope you find the Silver Bullet process to be your key to success, as so many others have.

To you, big brother Paul: I have, and always will, look up to you with great admiration and every day wish I could be more like you.

To you, G.A.: Even if you were not my brother, I would still choose you as my best friend.

Now that the writing is done, we realize that without these people supporting us, there would be no *Silver Bullet Selling*; it's funny how it takes a community to write a book.

G.A. Bartick
Paul Bartick
September 15, 2008

PART ONE

THIS IS SILVER BULLET SELLING

CHAPTER ONE

You Don't Have to Be a Natural-Born Salesman

BEEEEP BEEEEEP BEEEEP BEEEEP. I open one eye. The green numbers on my clock radio shout 3:00 A.M. "This sucks!" I think as I struggle to free one arm from the warmth of the covers and slap the snooze button. "Seven more minutes of blissful sleep, and then I'll get up." BEEEEP, BEEEEEP, BEEEEEP, BEEEEEEP. 3:07 A.M. "No . . . just one more snooze." Then reality hits . . . "I have to get up. I can't be late. I need this job. I need the money!" I can hear my wife's voice in my head: "We have bills to pay!"

For the past three months I have been waking up every morning at this godforsaken hour and crawling into my car to deliver the *Wall Street Journal* to a bunch of windbags who make more in one hour than I do in a week. After rolling, rubber-banding, and tossing 163 papers onto manicured lawns, I head back to our apartment. When I get back home at about 7:30, I am on kid duty because my wife Kelly is off to teach high school in southeast San Diego.

I plop my three-year-old daughter Alicia down in front of the TV while I shave, shower, and get dressed. Then I drag my sorry butt out of the house to drop her off at my in-laws' before heading off to my day job: G.A. Bartick, Mortgage Broker. Selling mortgages is what I'm supposed to be doing. It's a 100% commission job and I haven't closed a deal in over six weeks. I'm going broke being a broker. That's why I'm delivering papers at three in the frickin' morning for a hundred bucks a week. Kelly's teacher salary barely pays the rent.

Previously I had a nice job working for Nordstrom as a ladies' shoe salesman, but I wasn't that good at it. So I did what many salespeople do that aren't that good at sales—I went into management.

I spent over eight years learning Nordstrom's secrets about how customer service leads to great sales. Nordstrom is known as a great customer service organization, but don't kid yourself. It's a *sales* organization that uses fantastic customer service to generate over $8 billion in revenue annually. Nordstrom was a great training ground, but I had my eyes on loftier goals. I still believed I could make it big in the field of sales.

First I thought I could become rich selling real estate, so I studied, got my license, and got a job with Jelley Real Estate in Del Mar, California. "This is going to be great!" I thought. "I'm going to learn everything there is to know about the real estate market and people will buy from me!" Well, it didn't exactly turn out that way.

I was sitting at my desk on the last day of the month (which was also the last day of the pay period). My phone rang. It was my sales manager asking me to stop by his office at the end of the day. At 5:00 P.M., as I sat in his posh office, he told me he loved my attitude, my work ethic, and my product knowledge, but he'd been looking at the sales reports and I had only sold one house in the past six months. And then he said as he looked toward the door, "G.A., I'm sorry, it's just not working out."

So I soothed my bruised ego and, with my wife pushing me out the door, I set out to find another sales job. In about three weeks I got a job selling eyewear. I thought, "This is going to be fantastic! I'll learn everything there is to know about eyewear, and opticians, optometrists, and ophthalmologists will buy from me." Eight months into this gig the call came from my sales manager. "The call" always came on the last day of the pay period and, by now, I knew all too well what to expect. My managers all said the same thing: "I love your attitude. I love your work ethic and your product knowledge. But I have been looking at the sales reports and I'm sorry, G.A., it's just not working out."

That was 1996. Having a wife and a young child with another on the way, I had few options and even fewer sales skills. I was pounding the pavement every day and getting my butt kicked because I didn't know what I didn't know. I was really just winging it when it came to sales. I was selling on attitude, personality, and desire, without much to show for it. I was hunting without a bullet in the chamber and just shooting blanks. My gift of gab (yes, GAB are my initials) was no longer enough to help me reach the lofty personal and financial goals I had set for myself. Something had to give. We couldn't survive much longer on credit cards, and living in San Diego on Mrs. Bartick's pay as a teacher was not going to cut it. That's when I got the lucky phone call. It couldn't have come at a better time.

On the other end of the line was Michael St. Lawrence, Founder and President of a new sales consulting company named OutSell. Michael had just written the best-selling sales book *If You're Not Out Selling, You're Being Outsold*, and his fledgling company was taking off. Michael was the best friend of my brother Paul (the other author of this book), and he was calling because he was looking to hire training consultants with sales skills, success, and swagger. He knew about my desperate situation, so there was no use in stretching the truth. I told him I could certainly satisfy his swagger requirement, but wasn't so sure about the skills or success. After all, the sad truth was that I had failed in four prior sales jobs.

To my relief, Michael told me not to be too concerned about the lack of sales skills; he could teach me that part. In fact, he told me he knew my sales skills sucked and he was calling me because he was in a bit of a bind himself. He had just sold a huge training deal, but he didn't have the staff to deliver it. After a brief conversation on the phone and a follow-up face-to-face interview, he invited me to try out for OutSell. So I went to Marshalls department store and bought myself a new suit—on credit, of course—and gave it a shot.

I was one of 30 people trying out for 10 spots. There were professional speakers, facilitators, and sales professionals with impressive resumes and fancy degrees. I was way out of my league and was afraid of being embarrassed. We started on a Monday and for the next three days Michael led us through a sales boot camp. On Thursday I arrived early in order to work on a homework assignment we had been given the night before. Michael was in his office and he called me in "to have a little chat."

As I walked in to his office, I couldn't help thinking, "Here we go again: the death march." I knew the conversation with Michael would end with the words "I'm sorry, G.A., it's just not working out."

I really can't explain what happened next. Maybe it was because Michael was my brother's best friend or because I had known him from the day I was born, but somehow Michael saw the sales professional inside me and told me I had made the team—as long as I was willing to put in the hours to learn the sales skills I sorely lacked. Michael sat me down and explained to me that there are no shortcuts and no quick fixes and, most importantly, I had to learn the six basic steps of the sales process. I shook his hand enthusiastically and I've been a successful salesman ever since. As it turned out, those six steps changed my life.

$500 Sales Tip!

You don't close a sale, you open a relationship
—G.A. Bartick

CHAPTER TWO

I'm a Salesman and This Is My Story

Throughout the book I am going to relate true stories that illustrate my points. It's important that you understand my story because you need to know that, first and foremost, I am just like you. I am still out there picking up the phone, making cold calls, delivering sales presentations, getting objections, being told no over and over again, and I do all of this every day. I am not some snot-nosed California punk in a fancy custom suit taking in the action from my consultant's luxury box. I'm there in the trenches. My face is covered with blood, dirt, and grime from the battlefield. OutSell is a small company and we are out there in the marketplace doing battle with the big boys—the McKinseys and AchieveGlobals of the world—who have much fatter budgets and more fancy technology and teams full of buttoned-down sales consultants—and we're beating them.

Every day over the past 10 years I've been a living, breathing Silver Bullet Selling *fanatic*. To me, Silver Bullet Selling is code for creating a unique buying experience and building trusting relationships with my prospects and clients. I know the power of the process because I spent the first years of my sales career adrift in the sales wilderness without it.

I had no sales process.

I had no results.

I had no clue.

And in the end, I had no job.

That all changed when I committed to using a process and quit winging it.

What's in this book is the ammunition I needed years ago. In *Silver Bullet Selling* I have taken the age-old consultative sales method, enhanced it, and put it into a clear, concise process that you can execute in the field on your very next sales call.

During my career I've sold tens of millions of dollars of consulting, conducted thousands of sales calls with top professionals in dozens of industries, and trained more than 30,000 sales professionals. (By the time you read this, the number will be a whole lot bigger.) When I train and coach sales professionals and executives on the Bullet Selling process, I hear all the lame excuses why it won't work for them.

"My situation is different."

"G.A., you just don't understand *my* buyers."

"You've never sold <insert your product here> before!"

They test drive the Bullet Selling process for a few days and they fizzle because they judge its effectiveness before they ever become competent using it. Those who stick with the program for a couple of weeks start to see their performance improve, and those brave souls who push themselves to work the process until it becomes habit (i.e., roughly four weeks) swear by it just like I do.

What's in a Name?

Clients always ask me, "G.A. I need to know what to say to my prospects and clients so I can close more sales. I need to know what the silver bullet to sales is." I used to respond, "There is *no* silver bullet to sales. There is no one-liner or clever phrase you can say to your prospects that will open the heavens and magically close the sale for you. It's all about using a predictable and repeatable effective sales process." After saying this hundreds of times, though, I finally wised up and realized that the six-step sales process I've been teaching *is* the silver bullet. It is a straightforward, easily executed, extremely effective process. That's how it got its name . . . the Silver Bullet Selling process. I call it Bullet Selling for short.

Changing Lives Six Steps at a Time

What's in this book has changed careers and lives, including my own. Bullet Selling *is* the silver bullet to sales success. Six simple steps . . . so easy to learn . . . but let me be honest, it takes practice to become effective in its execution.

I'm not going to kid you; this stuff ain't easy. Sales ain't easy, and let's be thankful because if it was easy, everyone would do it and we wouldn't be paid as much. There is more money made in sales than in any other profession in the world. Another beautiful thing is that the Bullet Selling process will never be more difficult than it is today. As you study and practice Bullet Selling, it will become easier and you will become more successful.

If you're in sales, then your skill is communication. Bullet Selling is going to teach you to become even more skilled at communicating with your buyers. It is how to differentiate yourself from the competition. If you are not the low-cost leader, Bullet Selling shows you how to build value in the minds of your buyers. If you're going to be great in sales, you have to be a great communicator. Just as athletes, singers, and musicians must practice their skills, we salespeople must practice ours. Think of Bullet Selling as your sheet music to great sales.

I use, teach, and coach Bullet Selling as do the other consultants in our firm. I know the process works because I see it working every day with our clients. In fact, our work carries a 100% no-questions-asked, money-back guarantee (I guess I got that from my days at Nordstrom). Of the many thousands of standing-ovation performances we've delivered over the years, a client has exercised the guarantee only once and it wasn't because we didn't deliver results. (To read about this one occurrence, go to silverbulletselling.com.)

Knowing what to do and how to do it is not the same as effectively executing what needs to be done. This book will help you become effective at executing the skills of Bullet Selling. Do not, even for a second, confuse effort with results. Being successful is going to take effort, patience, and hard work. Reading *Silver Bullet Selling* is a good start, but it's not enough. You're going to have to take the skills you learn and apply them, practice them, and use them until they become part of your selling DNA.

CHAPTER THREE

Why You've Got to Read This Book

B ullet Selling is consultative selling at its best and then some. It refers to an interactive sales process that focuses on the buyer's needs rather than the sales professional's inventory.

The Six-Step Silver Bullet Selling Process

Bullet Selling requires you to work with the buyer toward a mutually beneficial solution, and it includes these six steps:

Step 1. Pre-Call Planning—Prepares you for a successful sales call.

Step 2. Building Rapport—Builds credibility and develops your relationship with the buyer.

Step 3. Discovery—Identifies the buyer's current situation, desired situation, expectations, and logical and emotional needs through a nonthreatening questioning model.

Step 4. Tailored Solution—Helps you design a customized solution or offer that bridges the buyer's current situation to his desired situation.

Step 5. Addressing Concerns—Handles buyer's concerns effectively so we can move the sale to a close.

Step 6. Closing the Sale—Asking for the order, recapping the transaction, and managing buyer expectations.

$500 Sales Tip!

Don't judge the Bullet Selling
process, or any process for that matter, until
you have used it in the field for 30 days.

—G.A. Bartick

There are already several brilliant books that describe the consultative sales process in detail, including Mack Hanan's classic *Consultative Selling* and Neil Rackham's *Spin Selling*. While these books are long on theory, they come up short on application. In other words, after reading one of these books, you'll definitely understand what consultative selling is, but you'll have no idea how to implement it in your daily sales activities. That's where *Silver Bullet Selling* comes in. We take the theory and show you how to apply it every day no matter what you are selling. Think of this book as a practical how-to guide that will put the Bullet Selling process to work for you on your very next sales call. This book is for you if you want to:

- Develop deeper, more loyal relationships with your buyers
- Make more sales
- Build your book of business
- Have more fun
- Earn more recognition
- Be promoted
- Win sales awards
- Increase your income

This book is for you no matter what you are selling, whether your sales cycle is 15 minutes or 15 months. *Silver Bullet Selling* is for sales professionals everywhere. It's for inside sales associates, outside sales reps, financial advisors, television producers, telemarketers, real estate agents, insurance agents, bankers, brokers, attorneys, product developers, medical sales reps, and anyone else who sells products, services, or ideas for a living. No matter what your business, it all begins with the interactions you have with your buyers and the way you communicate with them. Becoming an expert at Bullet Selling will allow you to maximize your impact and supercharge your success.

Who Wrote This Book Anyway?

We know sales. Every day of every week, OutSell consultants are criss-crossing the globe meeting, training, and coaching sales professionals. We have to convince VPs of sales, national sales managers, and boards of directors that they need to hire some buttoned-down, suited-up consultants to show them how to run their business even more effectively and to increase sales. And guess what? They say yes "Yes!" with enthusiasm. Why? Because we use the exact same proven sales process that we teach, Bullet Selling. And we deliver results and a *huge* return on investment for our clients.

By the time this book is published, we'll have taught the Bullet Selling process to more than 150,000 sales professionals. Through this constant exposure to sales professionals and sales organizations, we have continued to develop and refine the process so it is practical and easy to apply to real-life sales calls. This is not just fluff or filler.

Many good consultative/relationship-building sales models have been developed by some very good training companies (many of which are our competitors). Many of the key fundamentals we all talk about are similar, but as you'll see, what makes Bullet Selling unique is how we help you execute it on your very next sales call.

The six steps of the Bullet Selling process are the fundamentals of great sales, and the silver bullet is the execution. When you have a proven process that you can learn and immediately apply to what you do every day, you have a winning combination.

Every time we begin working with a new client, the first step of the project involves what we call "top producer discovery." We interview and observe their top-performing sales professionals and sales managers in the field to find out what they do that everyone else should be doing to create great results. We look at their skills, abilities, behaviors, activities, habits, and what they say and how they say it. Then we document it all and teach it to the rest of the organization; if more people are doing what top performers are doing, results will improve. It's really not rocket science, and it really works. This continuous exposure to the best and the brightest keeps us abreast of what creates top performance in sales. We are going to share these insights with you so that you too can learn to sell the way the most successful sales professionals sell.

Although this book taps into the collective wisdom, experience, and talent of our entire OutSell team, to make it easier on the reader, it will be told through my voice, G.A. Bartick, President of OutSell. Frequently we get together, brainstorm and organize everything we've learned through all of our practical in-the-field experience. We share stories of success and many of failure. Through this collaborative process we have distilled the sales process fundamentals into a complete how-to guide.

Our Research

We have over 36,000 pages of notes from interviews, interactions, and observations of more than 6,000 top-performing sales professionals and managers. Included in these pages are notes from interviews and observations of what some really poor sales professionals do. That's a lot of research. Think of 11 filing cabinets stuffed full with dog-eared, tattered notes from interviews and observations with sales professionals from dozens of industries including insurance, real estate, retail, banking, utilities, consumer durables, financial services, and telecommunications. This research is the gold we mine to develop our ideas and opinions. In fact, these 36,000 pages are the evidence we used to build the Bullet Selling process. I refer to this research throughout the book because I want to give you insights and tools that have been proven in the battlefield of real-world sales.

A Quick Note on Terminology

We've read many sales books and taken sales courses by some of the best in the business. In an attempt to be "original" and "unique," many of them developed different terms to describe the same concepts. Although they go to great lengths to describe the "huge" differences between "added value" and "value added," for example, we see through it. You will find no newly coined terms here.

In addition, different industries call buyers by different names. For instance, a financial services sales professional might call a buyer a client or prospect, while a technology services sales professional might call a buyer a buyer. To clarify all of this jargon, here are the words we use in this book.

> **Sales professional** = account executive = salesperson = salesman/woman = sales consultant = sales advisor = financial advisor = sales engineer = business development officer = agent = representative
>
> **Buyer** = client = customer = account = prospect
>
> **Bullet Selling** = six-step sales process
>
> *Silver Bullet Selling* = this book

When I talk about people who sell, I call them "sales professionals." When I talk about people who buy, I use "buyers." When I talk about our interactive sales process, I use "Bullet Selling." And when I refer to a sales professional or buyer or anyone else, I use the pronoun "he" rather than being politically correct and using "he/she."

Why I Wrote This Book

I wrote this book because I have seen all the rubbish that goes on out there—all the missed opportunities, all the low-hanging fruit that withered on the vine, all the sales that were right there for the taking if only the sales professionals had these six easy steps to help them open the relationship and close the sale.

I've made the same mistakes they've made. Over the years, I've learned that people make some of these mistakes simply because no one has shown them a truly effective process for communicating and selling. I want to spare you that long walk of shame from your desk to the boss's office to hear these painful words: "I'm sorry. It's just not working out" because I've been there.

How to Get the Most Out of This Book

If you are reading this book, you probably fit into one of two categories. You are either:

1. Loving life. You're selling a ton of your products, services, or ideas and making a lot of money doing it. You are a top producer for your company and in your industry, and you love your lifestyle. But you're looking to fine-tune your game because you know a little improvement can lead to dramatic results. That's why you're always looking for ways to improve.

2. Not doing as well as you would like. You are not a top producer yet. You know there are things that need to change about the way you sell in order for your results to improve. You have some great months and some not-so-great months. You want to become more consistent with your results and ultimately be more successful.

The common denominator for both of these categories is the desire to improve. *Silver Bullet Selling* will help you no matter which category you're in.

You are not going to read radically new ideas here because we simply haven't found a lot of radically new ideas that produce the same results as the ideas in this book. Some of what we present is obvious common sense. However, just because you've heard a fundamental before doesn't mean you're applying and executing it effectively every day. Nearly every American knows that a low-fat, high-fiber diet will improve health. This is an obvious fundamental. However, fewer and fewer people (myself included) apply this to the way they eat every day. This is why best seller lists contain new diet books every month. People want to believe there is an easier way when, in fact, the only way was, is, and always will be based on applying and executing proven fundamentals. Sorry, you can't pop a pill and become an effective sales professional.

It's important to understand that I am talking about incremental improvements here, not about dramatic changes in what you do. Yet getting just a little bit better at executing the fundamentals can lead to *huge* improvement in results. Bullet Selling will help you become a little bit more effective. It may be the feather that tips the scales your way. It may be what makes your next buyer say yes to you instead of your competition. It may be the difference between sales awards or those words I know so well, "It's just not working out."

So if you're ready, fasten your safety belt, put your seat and tray table in their full upright and locked positions, and take aim at the competition by turning the page and learning how to put *Silver Bullet Selling* to work for you!

CHAPTER FOUR

Why a Sales Process?

I hear it all the time: "G.A., I'm a natural. Sales come easy to me because of my personality. Why do I need to learn a sales process?" We all know the type: likable, outgoing, persuasive, smooth, enthusiastic. In fact, I thought I was one of them. But I'm not. I need a process.

Other people tell me, "Well, my situation is a little bit different, G.A. This all sounds good, but what you're talking about is not me. If I use a process, I'm going to sound canned or scripted. I have my own style and it works for me." If this sounds like you, you might be thinking "Do I really need this? Should I keep reading? I have so much other stuff I should be doing." Believe me, I've heard those same voices. And if you want my opinion, if you pick up just a few key points from this book, it could be worth millions of dollars to you over your career. Keep reading!

The Gift of Gab Doesn't Necessarily Translate into Sales Commissions

During my Nordstrom days, I was probably the friendliest sales associate on the floor. I intentionally engaged buyers in conversation and held court on the sales floor on any given afternoon. I was certain my enthusiasm and eager-to-help attitude would win me customers and sales commissions—and it did . . . some of the time.

One spring Saturday afternoon I was helping a regular customer of mine, Mrs. C, and her daughter Michelle, pick out some shoes for her high school graduation. I took the cue and started a conversation about finishing high school and summer vacation and college plans thereafter. The discussion hummed along as Michelle picked out some very nice fawn Ferragamo slingbacks. She loved the suppleness of the leather and the way they made her feet "sing." Michelle was also excited about how they would look with her dress. I asked Mrs. C and Michelle if they needed anything else before I rang them up and sent them on their way. It was a great interaction that left all three of us feeling good.

The very next afternoon when I arrived at work Mrs. C was waiting, this time with both of her daughters in tow. I straightened my tie, went up to them, and asked if everything was all right. Mrs. C assured me there was no problem and that she had returned to buy a pair of shoes for Michelle's sister. Before I could ask if they needed any help, my colleague Anthony came hustling out of the back room with a pair of Cole Haan open-toe pumps for her to try on. Obviously, Anthony had been helping them, so I retreated to the cash register to let him finish the sale. The store got busy so I started helping other buyers. About half an hour later I got a tap on my shoulder from Mrs. C, who was just leaving and wanted to say good-bye. To tell you the truth I was a little astonished she was still in the store. I thought maybe Anthony hadn't taken good care of her. I did a double take when I saw Mrs. C and her two daughters *each carrying three boxes of shoes.*

When the rush slowed and there was a break in the action, I asked Anthony how he had sold the women nine pairs of shoes. Anthony told me he followed a process that uncovered a lot of different "shoe needs," including prom, a Sweet 16 party, and a summer wedding among other events. He didn't explain exactly what the process was (I guess he didn't want to give away his competitive edge), but he did tell me that it certainly was the reason he was always near the top of the sales leader board. I was surprised that Anthony would follow a process; after all, he was gregarious and affable like me. I thought sales processes were for "sales sissies," people who lacked what I call a "sales personality." The sales process helped "them" compensate for their shortcomings. Honestly, to me the whole idea of a sales process was unsavory. I filed Anthony's words of wisdom away, and it wasn't until several years later that I understood what he was telling me.

Lowering Resistance and Raising Receptivity

The process Anthony was using was probably something like the Bullet Selling process. It must have generated a needs-based discussion while lowering buying resistance and increasing receptivity to what he had to say. That's what a great sales process does.

Keep in mind that the entire selling conversation makes people nervous. When you begin an interaction with a buyer, resistance is relatively high, even when he is looking to buy. Don't believe me? Just think about the last time you went into a store and an enthusiastic sales professional came up to you and asked, "Can I help you?" Did you feel a pang of queasiness in the pit of your stomach? A bit of tension in your shoulders? That, my friend, is resistance. We feel resistance because we don't want to be sold. We don't want some stranger coming up to us and selling us, even if we need and want what the person is selling! This is what makes the whole selling/buying puzzle so interesting. We all go into stores wanting to buy, but not wanting to be sold. That's why we tell that enthusiastic sales professional that we are "just looking."

But what if that enthusiastic sales professional was able to quickly strip away that sales resistance and help your natural desire to buy shine through? You would be more receptive to what he had to say, wouldn't you? That's the magic of the Bullet Selling process. It turns the selling interaction on its head. It takes the selling out of the equation by creating a *unique and different buying experience* for your buyer. How does it do this? That's a damned good question. I'm tempted to say just trust me, it works. But I don't think that would quite suffice here.

The Bullet Selling process works because it lowers buyers' resistance and raises their receptivity on purpose. It
EARNS
   YOU
      THE
         RIGHT
to engage in a business conversation. It gives you the opportunity to build your credibility and show your buyers they are in good hands. The process

enables you to build trust and, when your buyers begin to trust you, their resistance goes down and receptivity goes up. Remember, the entire Bullet Selling process is all about opening relationships and closing sales, and relationships are based on trust.

In Sales, Communication Is King

We've all heard the phrase "The customer is *king*." Well, fugetaboutit! When was the last time you tried to get some customer service from your phone company or utility? "Customer is king" went out with the mirror disco ball and polyester jump suit. Nowadays, *communication* is king in sales.

$500 Sales Tip!

Sales is a full contact communication sport.
—G.A. Bartick

In much the same way, to be successful in sales, you need to learn how to communicate effectively with your audience. Few of us have had the pleasure of working with a sales professional with truly excellent communication skills. We're talking about a professional who is able to communicate succinctly and effectively:

- What he does and how he does it
- His buyer's current situation, desired situation, and the tailored solution that will create the bridge between the two
- How his products and services benefit his buyer
- On-target, nonconfrontational responses to concerns
- A clear and persuasive close by asking for the order

The Bullet Selling process will help you become a much better communicator—and not just at work! It will help you develop what you want to say, how you want to say it, and even *when* you want to say it. If you follow the steps outlined in this book, you will get the practice you need to improve and refine your communication skills immediately.

Playing with Emotion

Another reason why the Bullet Selling process is so effective has to do with satisfying buyers' emotional and logical needs. Regardless of the situation, emotional and logical needs influence the decisions we make, especially buying decisions. People make buying decisions for a variety of reasons. For example, the typical TV shopper spends more than 20 hours researching the myriad of available products. That same person might make a very quick decision about one of life's most important decisions—perhaps the person he will marry or how to invest for retirement—based on instinct or emotion. Another person might spend weeks, months, or years analyzing the situation to make the same decision. To be successful with a wide variety of buyers, we need to be able to appeal to both their emotional and logical needs. There's an old saying in sales—"We rationalize with logic what we want emotionally"—and that is certainly true for most people. At least I know it's true with me.

——— ——— ———

So there I was at a department store trying on a new suit in front of one of those three-way mirrors. You know, the kind that shows every single imperfection (and for me, the mirrors have plenty to show). As I stood there, a young lady walked by and said, "Boy, that suit sure makes you look thin." I immediately turned to my sales professional and said, "I'll take it." When I got home, I said to my wife, "Hey, honey, look at my new suit. I got it . . . on sale!" I bought the suit because it made me look thin (emotional need) and rationalized the purchase by saying I bought it on sale (logical need).

Many sales professionals are satisfied with addressing their buyers' logical needs only. Danger lurks here. Buyers whose emotional needs are not met usually end up being former buyers. Here's a case in point.

Over winter break my family and I were visiting my mother in northern California. Mom gave my daughter Alicia a pair of pajamas as a gift, but they were a size too big. So the next day we headed to the mall to exchange them. We went into the store and I found the exact same pair of PJs in her size. I took both pairs up to the register, said hello to the store associate, and told her my situation. She immediately uttered those famous words: "Do you have your receipt?" Yes, in fact I did, and I presented it to her. She rang up the transaction and after a few moments she turned to me and said, "That will be $5.97." I was a little surprised. I said, "They're the same pajamas. Why do I owe you any money? Isn't it an even exchange?" "Well, sir, these were originally purchased on sale, and now they're at regular price. And the difference is $5.97. If you purchase something on sale and then exchange it, you have to pay the difference between the sales price and the regular price. That is store policy."

I took issue with that because of my Nordstrom background. Good customer service would dictate that this should be an even exchange. Don't you agree? So what did I do? I asked to speak to the manager! As the manager came over to talk to me, I saw my mom, wife, and three kids slowly backing away. They knew a confrontation was coming. I calmly explained the situation to the manager, who supported his associate and said, "Yes, that is store policy. You see, what if you purchased it at regular price and it was now on sale? You would want us to pay you back the difference, wouldn't you?"

And I said, "Yes, you're right. If I bought it at regular price and it went on sale within a reasonable period of time, say 30 days or less, I think good customer service calls for the store to refund me the difference."

He considered this for a moment and then shot back, "Sir, this time and this time only we will do an even exchange." Then he pointed his finger at me. "But next time, if you purchase something on sale and need to exchange it, you will owe us the difference."

Were my logical needs met? Yes. I got my daughter a pair of pajamas in her size as an even exchange.

Were my emotional needs met? Not at all. I was hoping the store would treat me as a valued buyer, not as a "policy breaker." A little understanding and empathy would have kept me as a buyer, but I haven't stepped foot in that store since.

— — —

Here's the big thing about emotional and logical needs. Pay close attention because this is something you can use in everyday life. Sales professionals often complain, "Well, I fixed their problem, why are they still mad?" Why? Because you only took care of part of the total deal. If you only fix the problem, then you only met their logical needs. The buyers' emotional needs are still unresolved, and often emotional needs are as important as, if not more important than, logical needs. If you can address both needs, you'll be a lot more effective as a sales professional.

Sometimes you can't fix the problem and take care of your buyers' logical needs. In these situations, can you still leave buyers feeling good by taking care of only their emotional needs? Absolutely. We cannot always take care of our buyers' logical needs, but we almost always can take care of their emotional needs, and this will leave buyers feeling better about the interaction and about us.

— — —

One of my colleagues doesn't exactly love to fly. (He's in good company. More than one in four Americans share his aerophobia, or fear of flying, which makes it the third most common phobia.)

He was flying from Newark, New Jersey, to a meeting in Detroit, Michigan, the next day. It was the dead of winter, and there was a monster nor'easter bearing down on the New York metropolitan area. This certainly did not ease his nerves. What made matters worse was that he was delayed in traffic and arrived at the airport

Did you know...

The two most common phobias are: arachnophobia and fear of public speaking.

only 27 minutes before the departure time. He ran through the terminal, zipped through security (luckily the line was short), and even hailed a ride on a motorized cart that whisked him to his gate. When he got there, the agent told him the flight was overbooked and that his seat had already been assigned to someone else. Now my colleague wasn't just nervous, he was mad! He raised his voice and explained to the agent that he was a platinum frequent flyer and how important it was that he get on that plane. The agent apologized several times and told him he would help him if he could, but the flight had already boarded and was full.

Then the agent took control of the situation. Instead of sending my colleague to the customer service line, he took care of him right there. He booked him on the next direct flight out and put him in first class. The agent even gave him a day pass to the frequent flyer club so he could relax while he waited the three hours for his plane. My colleague composed himself, apologized for his behavior, and thanked the agent. Although the agent wasn't able to satisfy my colleague's logical needs, he did take care of his emotional needs, and my friend was very grateful.

In this true story the agent took care of my friend's emotional needs by owning the situation and sincerely apologizing to my colleague. Most of the time listening and apologizing are all it takes.

CHAPTER FIVE

What Is This Bullet Selling Process, Anyway?

If you're like me, you've heard enough chatter and are ready to see, feel, and test drive the process. So on with it!

The Bullet Selling process helps us succeed on purpose. It is not a collection of suggestions, tips, or random recommendations we came up with in the company War Room. Rather, it is a collection of best practices from top performers from dozens of industries, distilled down into a proven six-step process. This stuff really works. That's why we've trained 10 of the Fortune 50 companies to use it every day. The process helps build the foundation for a solid relationship in a systematic and predictable way. We call it the Bullet Selling process because it is the closest thing we know to a no-fail sales system. We know it works—we use it ourselves—and that's why we guarantee it with all our consulting clients.

$500 Sales Tip!

Sales success comes from two things: telling a great story, and telling it to enough people.

—G.A. Bartick

We use the six-step process whether we're meeting a new prospect for the first time or a veteran buyer for the fortieth. Understand that it's not an inflexible process that standardizes every buyer interaction. Rather, it's a *framework* that provides a structure for every interaction. Each step of the Bullet Selling process builds on the previous step and is designed to help you move toward the target (a "Yes!" from your buyer). So let's take a look at the six steps.

The Six Steps: An Overview

In Chapter 3 I introduced the six steps of the Bullet Selling process. Now we're going into more detail.

Step 1. Pre-Call Planning

Before we can pick up the phone or go on an appointment, we have to do a little pre-call planning. This 15- to 30-minute activity can make all the difference. It includes everything we should do to prepare for the sales call. The more prepared we are, the more confident and relaxed we'll be. Being confident and relaxed will allow us to be more effective, increasing our probability of success. I believe the outcome of any meeting can be predicted simply by the amount of pre-call planning that happens before the meeting.

Step 2. Building Rapport

Often the first few minutes of any buyer interaction determines how the rest of the meeting will go. At the beginning of an interaction buyer resistance is usually high, so it's important to build rapport and trust quickly to reduce resistance and increase receptivity.

Step 3. Discovery

The Bullet Selling process is all about understanding our buyers' needs and then providing a tailored solution that will help them meet their goals. Whether you sell kitchen appliances or financial products, the Discovery step allows you to understand your buyers' needs through a logical questioning flow that covers their:

- Current situation
- Desired situation
- Expectations of you and your product/service

Step 4. Tailored Solution

An effective discovery will arm you with your buyers' current and desired situation, along with their expectations of you, your product, and your company. Now it's time to design a customized solution that will create the bridge between where they are currently and where they want to be. The Tailored Solution step is your opportunity to present the features and benefits of the products/services you offer and a compelling reason why your buyers should do business with you.

Step 5. Addressing Concerns

Overcoming buyer concerns is a natural part of the selling process. Concerns come from fear, doubt, skepticism, and emotional reactions to the entire buying conversation. The greatest idea in the world often meets with some resistance before it is accepted and acted upon, and sales professionals need a step-by-step process to help buyers make a positive buying decision. The Bullet Selling process addresses concerns in a nonconfrontational way to bring buyers' objections into the open. Then you can respond to their concerns in a way that increases the likelihood of buyers doing business with you.

Step 6. Closing the Sale

Closing is the natural conclusion at the end of the Bullet Selling process. However, if we blow it during the Pre-Call Planning, Building Rapport, Discovery, Tailored Solution, or Addressing Concerns steps, no high-powered closing technique will save us at the end. We must get into the habit of asking for our buyers' business in an effective way. When done properly, closing actually opens the door to satisfied buyers who will want to do more business with you and refer business to you as well.

Auxiliary Firepower: Part 3

There is more to selling than the face-to-face (or phone-to-phone) conversation. Throughout the book and especially in Part 3, I provide additional ammunition to help you create success on purpose. The Bullet Selling Asking for Referrals process, the Bullet Selling (Net)Working the Room process, and Time Management Fundamentals are three additional bullets you will be armed with in Part 3.

Our Map to Success: The Bullet Selling Process

If you were planning to drive across the country, what are the three most important things you would take with you? Music to pass the time . . . probably. Cell phone to stay connected to the outside world (your buyers) . . . certainly. A GPS system to map your course and help you find your way across the deserts and mountains . . . definitely. Think of the Bullet Selling process as your sales GPS. It will keep you on course so you can accomplish your goals.

Great Sales: One Part Process, One Part Personality

I opened Chapter 4 with a question I hear all the time. "G.A., I'm a natural. Sales come easy to me because of my personality. Why do I need to learn a sales process?" From what you've read over the past two chapters, I hope you have a powerful answer at the ready, but let me make it perfectly clear. The Bullet Selling process makes you a better sales professional. It allows you to create success on purpose and generate consistently excellent results because it:

- Lowers buyers' resistance and raises receptivity and trust
- Helps you develop excellent communication skills
- Satisfies buyers' logical and emotional needs
- Sets you apart from the competition

- Creates more perceived value for your product/service
- Enables you to close more sales

And all this adds up to earning more income.

However, I am the first to admit that the Bullet Selling process is not the be-all and end-all. By itself, the process is lifeless. From the thousands of interviews and sales interactions I've been involved with, it has become abundantly clear that there are two parts to great sales: One part is process and one part is personality. Bullet Selling is the process. To make it truly effective, you need to add your personality. The most successful users of the Bullet Selling process are those who have paid the price in time, energy, and effort to learn each step. They practice the steps until they become proficient at the process, then they insert their own personality into it. That's when the Bullet Selling process becomes a part of their sales DNA.

It's a Process, Not a Script

Remember that Bullet Selling is not a script. This point is important because understanding the process allows you to be flexible and to customize it to each sales situation. What you say may change, but the process should not. It's the process that converts good salespeople into great sales professionals because it gives them the ability to repeat their success over and over again. Think about how many buyer conversations you have each day, each week, each month. What would happen if you could become just a little bit more effective? If you could convert just 5% more of your opportunities into sales, how much additional income would that put into your wallet?

Here's a fun exercise that illustrates how using a process can make you more effective.

Step 1. Look at this key for 10 seconds and try to memorize it.

⌐ = 1

⊔ = 2

∟ = 3

⌐ = 4

□ = 5

⌐ = 6

⌐ = 7

⌐ = 8

⌐ = 9

Step 2. Without peeking at the key, go ahead and solve these two equations in 30 seconds:

$$\sqcup \ + \ \sqsubset \ - \ \llcorner \ =$$

$$\sqsupset \ - \ \llcorner \ + \ \lrcorner \ =$$

Step 3. Now look at this key for 2 seconds.

1	2	3
4	5	6
7	8	9

Step 4. Again, without looking back at the key, solve these two equations in 10 seconds:

$$\square \ + \ \sqsubset \ - \ \llcorner \ =$$

$$\urcorner \ - \ \llcorner \ + \ \lrcorner \ =$$

Did you have an easier time of it using a process? The power of a process is that it leads to predictable results and makes you much more effective.

A Little More Effectiveness Leads to Dramatic Results

As proof that becoming just a little more effective can lead to dramatic results, take a look at the PGA results for 2005. Tiger Woods and Phil Mickelson each entered 21 tournaments. Tiger's average round for 18 holes was 68.66 strokes. Phil's average was 69.39 strokes, a mere .73 strokes behind. This means that in a round of 18 holes, they would play dead even for the first 17. Then on the 18th hole Tiger would be less than 1 stroke better. But being just a little bit better certainly led to dramatic differences on the money board. Tiger earned $10,628,023 to Phil's $5,699,605—that's 86% more prize money for Tiger. He was less than a stroke better, but almost doubled Phil's earnings.

Imagine what would happen to your income if you stopped winging it, embraced the Bullet Selling process, and became just a little more effective on your very next selling interaction!

PART TWO

SIX-STEP BULLET
SELLING PROCESS

Pre-Call Planning

1. **Pre-Call Planning**
2. Building Rapport
3. Discovery
4. Tailored Solution
5. Addressing Concerns
6. Closing the Sale

CHAPTER SIX

Pre-Call Planning Overview

Thorough pre-call planning gives me the confidence and clarity of focus I need to run through walls.

—G.A. Bartick

Pre-Call Planning Defined

Q: What is pre-call planning?

A: Pre-call planning is the work we do to prepare for a sales call with a buyer. We do this preparation before every sales call, and it can have an enormous impact on what happens during the call. Pre-call planning varies from industry to industry and can involve quick research or entire projects. In some businesses, such as pharmaceuticals and engineering, preparing for a sales call can take weeks of work. In other businesses, especially those that are transactional, such as telesales, sales professionals have only seconds to get ready for their next call.

Q: Why is pre-call planning so important?

A: Because it helps us close more sales. No matter what industry we work in, we need to do pre-call planning because it is the first step to generating success on purpose.

The Importance of a Quiet Mind

Pre-call planning is all about walking into an appointment or phone call with a buyer and being totally prepared for and focused on the job at hand. When you're prepared, you're confident and proactive. Pre-call planning includes everything you should do to prepare for a meeting from attire to directions to research to practice. The more prepared you are for the appointment, the more effective the meeting will go, increasing your probability of success.

$500 Sales Tip!

We've run more than 10,000 sales meetings and have found that the best predictor of the meeting's outcome is the pre-call planning that happens before the meeting.
—G.A. Bartick

Have you ever rushed to an appointment or arrived ill prepared? If you're like me, in these situations you arrive with a noisy and unfocused mind instead of feeling calm and in charge. My mind is racing and I'm thinking about things that won't help my performance, such as "Will she be able to tell that I don't know much about her industry?" or random thoughts like "Do I need to pick up my dry cleaning today or can I go another day without it?" or "What questions do I need to ask, and what information do I need to gather?" When I'm not prepared, I'm off my game and I'm fooling myself to think it won't affect my performance during the meeting.

I hate that feeling and want to avoid it at all costs. Pre-call planning is my remedy. That's why I do whatever possible to prepare for meetings. I even go so far as doing a drive-by the day before just to make sure I know where I'm going. To me, a noisy mind is an invitation for trouble.

Being well prepared for a meeting puts me in the zone. I'm laser-focused on the buyer and the meeting. In my zone I find comfort, confidence, creative energy, and success. Given the choice—and I almost always have a choice—I'll do the pre-call planning necessary to create a quiet mind.

Could You Be Better . . .

At Pre-Call Planning?

Could you be better at . . .

Y   N   Preparing yourself for your sales calls?

Y   N   Increasing your knowledge by researching your buyers or industry?

Y   N   Identifying the objective(s) of a sales call before meeting with buyers?

Y   N   Developing an agenda for a sales call?

Y   N   Making a professional and competent impression?

Y   N   Preparing for your sales calls by rehearsing what you're going to say?

Y   N   Making more sales?

A Bullet from G.A.'s Chamber

There I was on a business trip in Modesto, California. With my appointments done for the day and nowhere else to go, I decided to drop off the rental car and go to the airport early to get some work done. Now, Modesto's a nice small town in California's Central Valley, about 90 miles from San Francisco. The airport is so small the parking is still free! I dropped off my rental car and walked into the terminal. I checked my bag with the ticket agent and she informed me they were not ready for passengers to enter the boarding area yet.

So I settled down in a chair in the foyer to do some work. After about an hour the battery on my laptop ran dry and that's when I realized I had left the AC power cord at home. With nothing else to do I decided to relax and watch the activity around me. From where I sat I could see through the boarding area and right out onto the tarmac. A few minutes later, I heard the hum of an approaching twin-engine puddle-jumper coming in for a landing. FYI, I am not a big fan of small planes. As I watched the plane land I noticed that the ticket agent who checked my bag was now out on the tarmac wearing one of those reflector vests and signaling with a pair of those orange flashlights. To my surprise, she was out there directing the plane to the gate. This revelation didn't do much to quell my building anxiety.

> ## Did you know...
>
> George Lucas was born in Modesto, California and set his film classic *American Graffiti* there.

I watched as the ticket agent/landing technician helped the pilot park the plane. Moments later I saw her driving a luggage tractor next to the plane and she started unloading the baggage. I'm telling you, this is a small airport! The passengers then disembarked, followed by the crew. About 10 minutes later, there she was again. The ticket agent/landing technician/baggage handler was now in the boarding area, ready to operate the x-ray machine and metal detector. She motioned for me and the other 18 or so passengers to proceed through the metal detector and into the boarding area. Once in the boarding area, my head was on a swivel. I was looking back and forth, back and forth between the empty cockpit of the plane and the ticket agent/landing technician/baggage handler/boarding agent. I'm thinking that just maybe she was going to fly the plane, too!

A few minutes later, to my relief, a pilot showed up and hustled down the ramp to the tarmac. He looked rather young and took what appeared to be a checklist from his portfolio. I watched anxiously as he spent the next five minutes walking around the plane opening hatches, checking parts of the plane, and marking things on his checklist. I was quite certain the pilot was a rookie; why else would he need a checklist? A seasoned pilot would have this stuff memorized!

More than a bit concerned, I boarded the plane. I caught the attention of the fresh-faced pilot as I passed the cockpit and questioned him about his checklist. To my surprise, I learned that he had been flying for the past 13 years. When I asked him about the checklist, he told me the FAA requires all pilots to use a detailed preflight checklist to make sure the plane is flight-ready. Then he winked at me and said, "You wouldn't want me to forget something now, would you?"

His answer was perfect. Relieved, I took my seat and spent the ninety minute flight to San Diego handwriting my own preflight packing checklist, including everything I need to pack before a business trip (see the actual list on the next page). At the very top is "computer & charger."

$500 Sales Tip!

If a preflight checklist is good enough for a commercial pilot, then a pre-call checklist is good enough for me.

—G.A. Bartick

I made this list back in 2002 and I still use it before every business trip I take. I swear by it because it takes less than a minute to check and I never forget anything (as long as I remember to check it!).

G.A. Bartick Preflight Checklist

Accessories:

☐ Computer & charger	☐ MP3 player
☐ Earphones	☐ Book
☐ Cell phone & charger	☐ Cell phone headset

Toiletries:

☐ Toothbrush	☐ Hair spray
☐ Toothpaste	☐ Cologne
☐ Floss	☐ Contacts
☐ Hairbrush	☐ Contact solution
☐ Shaving cream	☐ Pills
☐ Razor	☐ Puffer
☐ Hair gel	☐ Nail clipper

Clothes:

☐ Suits	☐ Dress shirts
☐ Belt	☐ Ties
☐ Dress socks	☐ White socks
☐ Dress shoes	☐ Tennis shoes
☐ Underwear	☐ Collar stays
☐ Watch	☐ Wedding ring

CHAPTER SEVEN

What Pre-Call Planning Really Means

Pre-Call Planning Means Research

For some of us, pre-call planning means research. We may have to research articles, review web sites, or simply get on the phone and start doing detective networking. Different sales professionals do it in different ways, including:

Did you know...

A 10-K report is the official annual business and financial report filed by public companies with the Securities and Exchange Commission.

- Reading various company communications like annual reports, 10-K reports, letters to shareholders, and press releases
- Searching the Internet for relevant news and information about the company and industry
- Requesting and reviewing company brochures about products and services
- Checking the company's web site for information about personnel, performance, products, and recent announcements
- Asking a stockbroker or analyst for company performance reports or insights

The key here is to familiarize yourself with the company and culture you are calling on so you can discuss relevant issues and ask intelligent questions. You need to understand the issues facing the industry and how you have solved those issues for other buyers. Doing this not only prepares you to respond effectively during the call, but it also creates a favorable impression on the buyer by highlighting your preparation and professionalism.

Early on in my career at OutSell, I went on a sales call to a large wire house in San Francisco. I had just completed a project for another brokerage firm that went very well, and I felt confident that I knew the industry and this particular company. So I didn't need to do any pre-call planning.

Did you know...

The Wilshire 5000 Index measures the performance of publicly traded companies based in the United States. The index includes nearly all common stocks, real estate investment trusts, and limited partnership shares traded primarily on the New York Stock Exchange, Nasdaq, and American Stock Exchange.

On this particular call, I was seeing a Senior Vice President about a performance improvement project. During the first 10 minutes of the meeting, he repeatedly referred to the Wilshire 5000. Assuming it was company-specific jargon, I politely said, "I'm sorry, but I'm not familiar with the Wilshire 5000." Stupid! If he had an ejector button, he would have immediately launched me into orbit. Instead, he stood up and said, "You obviously aren't ready to be meeting with me and I'm pretty busy, so why don't we end this meeting now." I knew he was right so, without saying another word, I gathered my things and sheepishly walked out of his office. Needless to say, I never made a sale to that firm, but the lesson I learned was very valuable: Do your homework before you walk into the appointment.

Pre-Call Planning Definitely Means Appearance

I hear you whining "Not another dress-for-success lecture!" Okay, I'll keep it short, but you've got to read it because it is extremely important. On every call, sales professionals should try to make a favorable visual impression. In general, we make a better impression with a professional, clean, and conservative appearance. At OutSell we like to say that we "dress in the center of the envelope. We don't push the envelope." A variety of studies have been conducted and books written about the impact of clothing and appearance on credibility, perceived competence, trustworthiness, and even likability. If you want to make a stellar impression, look the part.

Dress to Reflect Your Values

I don't know about you, but I've heard a lot about dressing to reflect your buyer. I absolutely disagree. I dress to reflect the values that I want my buyers to see in me. That's why I wear the highest-quality clothes I can afford. For me, it means always being in a suit and tie, though I sometimes work with sales professionals who are wearing T-shirts.

Since it's important to me to look my very best, I am always visiting the tailor. Suits that I bought just a year ago might not fit as well today, so I have them regularly nipped and tucked (in my dreams . . . in reality, mostly I have them let out).

Nearly all of the successful women in sales we have talked to agree that it is best for women to dress conservatively, with tasteful jewelry and makeup. Hair is generally best when it is pulled back and not in need of constant "hair flips" to move runaway strands out of the eyes. Hair flips look great in slow motion on the movie screen, but not in sales meetings.

The business of personal appearance also holds true for you "creatives" out there. My brother Paul used to be a TV producer and writer, and he found that dressing well helped him close more deals.

I realize that appearance is not an easy topic to agree on because tastes and personal preferences really differ. Just understand that dressing for success when going to a social event—say a party, a date, or a basketball game—is completely different from dressing for success at a business event like a sales call or a networking mixer. It is also possible to be overdressed. A fashionable euro-suit with big lapels and boysenberry stripes right out of GQ might not be appropriate for business.

Getting There on Time Is Pre-Call Planning

I love our book agent, Martha Jewett. I knew she was right for us when, early in our relationship, she shared some words to live by from her grandmother: "If you're not early, you're late." I am fanatically punctual. Being late is disrespectful and totally unacceptable. That's why my colleagues know that if I'm late, something out of the ordinary must have happened.

Blast from the Past!

Give me six hours to chop down a tree and I
will spend the first four sharpening the axe.
—Abraham Lincoln

I go to great lengths to be on time. As I told you earlier, when I go to an unfamiliar city, I do a dry run by driving from the hotel to the office building or wherever I am conducting business the next day. I do this even when I rent a car with a navigation system. I don't trust those things to work every time.

Part of it is my paranoia and part of it is the fact that I was born without "navigational DNA." My sense of direction is seriously impaired.

Navigating to an appointment isn't the only potential hiccup, how-ever. One of my biggest fears is oversleeping for a meeting. Too many times the hotel operator doesn't make the wakeup call. Too many times the clock was set for P.M., not A.M. Too often before a big meeting I have woken up five or six times in a cold sweat because I dreamt I had overslept. By the time morning comes, I'm a wreck. Has this ever happened to you?

I remedy this with redundancy. I have a no-fail system:

1. Set the room alarm clock (double-check A.M./P.M.).
2. Schedule a wakeup call with the hotel front desk.
3. Set my cell phone alarm.
4. And if it's a super-important meeting, I call my mom and have her call to wake me up. She hates it when I'm on the East Coast and ask for a 5 A.M. (ET) wakeup call from her, but I don't dare ask my wife, Kelly. She is busy taking care of our three kids, three greyhounds, three guinea pigs, and Otis, my tortoise. When I ask her to wake up at 2 A.M. to call and make sure I'm up, she laughs and says, "I guess you're going to be late."

By now you probably realize that I have some inner demons I have to deal with every day. Being G.A. Bartick is no easy task.

Rehearsing Is Pre-Call Planning

I'm going to repeat over and over again how important it is to actually practice what you're going to say. Remember that sales is a full-contact communication sport and we have to constantly sharpen our communi-cation skills.

As you already know, I once sold eyeglasses to optometrists and other eye-care professionals. When I began, my supervisor took me out for a day on his sales calls to show me how it was done. We arrived 15 minutes early for the first appointment. My boss parked the car and sat quietly staring forward. After three minutes in this trance-like state, he told me he was ready to go. During the meeting, I was impressed with how articulate he was and how well he communicated our eye-wear's competitive advantage. For the second appointment, we also arrived 15 minutes early. Again my boss parked the car and assumed the trance position. After a couple of minutes, I gathered the courage to ask what he was doing. He told me he was rehearsing in his mind, going over what he was going to tell the buyer and how he was going to handle his concerns. He explained that he needed to practice his process to stay sharp, even after 17 years of selling. He said he usually did his rehearsing out loud, but did not want to scare me off on my first day.

Pre-Call Planning in Team Selling Situations: The 10 Key Issues

A lot of sales organizations, including ours, use the team approach to sales. Pre-call planning is even more essential in team selling situations because you have to coordinate so you make a seamless presentation to your buyers. We often have two or three colleagues meet with a potential buyer. Before the meeting we always get together, in person or via conference call, to address 10 key issues:

1. Define what success looks like at the end of the meeting.
2. Assign roles and responsibilities, including meeting leader, support, and note-taking scribe.
3. Develop the agenda for the meeting.
4. Decide what collateral we need and who is going to bring it.
5. Explore what obstacles and/or concerns we are likely to face.
6. Discuss who will respond and how to best respond to each concern.
7. If we are going to ask buyers to change vendors or the way they do business, do we know the benefit to them?

8. Can we articulate why they should change?

9. What additional resources might be needed?

10. What are the next steps going to be?

$500 Sales Tip!

Defining what success looks like is one of the
most important fundamentals of running
effective meetings. Before the meeting, we need
to understand what we are trying to accomplish
and then set the agenda with items that will
help us accomplish it efficiently.

— G. A. Bartick

Addressing each of these 10 issues is a great start to creating success on purpose.

NOTE: *If I'm going into a sales call solo, I address these same 10 issues as part of my pre-call planning. In fact, these questions are so important to me that I have them printed on the bottom of our OutSell notepads.*

When does pre-call planning usually happen? On the car drive over or in the buyer's lobby, right? This is *not* planning for success.

A 30-minute pre-call planning meeting back at the office or on the phone with your team is *huge*! I've been in meetings when, just as if on cue, the buyer raises the "cost" concern. Then my colleague addresses the concern just as we had practiced during our pre-call planning meeting. There is nothing more beautiful than when a meeting with a buyer runs like a well-oiled machine.

I know we're all "meetinged" to death, and this pre-call planning meeting seems like an easy one to blow off. Don't! Can the buyer tell when you and your team are not well prepared? You betcha!

Getting the Names Right Is Pre-Call Planning

No matter what you're selling, getting people's names right is important. On most sales calls, you'll be meeting people for the first time. More and more companies are using teams to make buying decisions, and that means you could be meeting up to a dozen people (and sometimes more) for the first time. If you have difficulty remembering names, ask your contact to tell you the names of anyone who will be sitting in on your sales call. This will give you the opportunity to write the names down and review them prior to your meeting. Nothing is more embarrassing than forgetting the name of a buyer and trying to avoid saying anything that might cause you to have to use that person's name. Believe me, I've done it. It's okay to take that sheet of paper into the meeting with you. That way, when you forget someone's name and want to address them during the meeting, you've got your cheat sheet ready.

━━ ━━ ━━

Remembering names is a learned skill. I'm proof of that. I used to have a terrible time with names. Kent McDougall, an OutSell colleague, happens to be amazing with names. When I walk into a buyer's office with Kent, he'll be calling everyone by name, including the security guard and receptionist. It's fun to watch and I wanted Kent to teach me the secret. I wasn't surprised when I learned that the secret is a simple three-step process. The true test came when I was introducing myself and the Bullet Selling process to a 24-member senior executive team for Nevada State Bank. I started the meeting by setting an agenda and then had everyone introduce themselves. After the final executive spoke, I went around the room and addressed everyone by their name. They broke into spontaneous applause. Talk about building rapport! The Silver Bullet Name-Remembering process has three steps:

Step 1. Listen

You have to hear the person's name. So right before you meet someone, clear your mind and really concentrate on simply hearing his name.

Step 2. Name Association

As you hear the name, make an association—the sillier the better. For example, let's play with my name: G.A. Bartick. I'm a pretty good guy, so you may think of the G.A. as "Good Apple." Then for Bartick, think of a big, fat tick leaning up against a bar. So, there you have it. Picture me as a **G**ood **A**pple and I am leaning up against the **bar** next to a **tick**. Silly, yes. Effective, yes!

Step 3. Repetition

Repeat the name in your mind along with the association. And use his name a few times during the conversation, but don't overdo it.

I teach this process in my classes, and everyone is amazed at how well it works. Once you get good at it, you can memorize the names of 20 people in as little time as it takes for them to introduce themselves.

Pre-Call Planning Is Ironing Your Briefcase

Many times I've been in a sales meeting and needed a form or other document. So I reached into my briefcase and pushed aside the mints, the loose change, the candy wrappers, and surprise . . . it's not there.

That's why every night at around 10, after all the e-mails are answered and just before the lights go out, I "iron my briefcase." I do this exercise religiously because it helps me to relax, knowing that I am ready for the next day. "Ironing my briefcase" means reviewing my schedule for the next day and making sure I have all the materials I'll need. Here's what you do:

1. Review calendar and schedule.
2. Empty the contents of your briefcase and file everything you don't need.
3. Collect all the materials (e.g., order forms, new account forms, ACAT forms, brochures, notepad, samples, pitch book, etc.) you need for the next day and put them neatly in your briefcase.

Ironing helps you take the wrinkles out of tomorrow by preparing today.

$500 Sales Tip!

The most obvious symptom indicating a
need for better planning is the feeling
that we are simply too busy to spend
time planning.

—G.A. Bartick

CHAPTER EIGHT

Pre-Call Planning Checklists

Examples: Pre-Call Planning Checklists

In this chapter we provide pre-call planning checklists from several different industries. The more extensive and complete your checklist, the better off you'll be. You may not use every item on every call, and that is just fine. I believe the best checklist is the one you build and customize yourself.

Click Here!
We've posted more examples of checklists from different industries at www.silverbulletselling.com.

Financial Services

✓

_____ Research the industry/company using available research tools, First Research, client web site, Salesgenie.com

_____ Read white papers on the industry and market trends

_____ Address the 10 key issues

_____ Define the purpose of the meeting

_____ Define what success looks like

_____ Develop the agenda for the meeting

_____ Bring materials and collateral

_____ Identify potential obstacles and how to overcome them

_____ Identify potential concerns buyer might have and how to respond

_____ Identify additional resources that might be needed

_____ Practice credibility statement

_____ Practice discovery questions

_____ Practice banking philosophy

_____ Bring pitch book and other presentation tools

_____ Bring all forms (new account, ACAT, order)

_____ Prepare to ask for referrals

_____ Anticipated next steps

NOTE: *Later chapters cover the credibility statement, discovery questions, and banking philosophy.*

Wholesalers

✓

_____ Plan to be on time

_____ Dress to reflect success and professionalism

_____ Practice sales process

_____ Address the 10 key issues

_____ Define purpose of visit

_____ Define what success looks like

_____ Develop agenda

_____ Bring current catalog, materials, collateral, and samples

_____ Review hard route and/or delivery schedule

_____ Client file: Review notes from previous visit and sales history

_____ Review initiatives and promotions

_____ Organize day planner, order forms, and scorecard

_____ Fill out route on daily sales activity report

_____ Organize vehicle

_____ Review current client commitments

_____ Identify potential obstacles and how to overcome them

_____ Identify potential concerns buyer might have and how to respond

_____ Identify additional resources that might be needed

_____ Practice credibility statement

_____ Practice discovery questions

_____ Practice business philosophy

_____ Bring presentation tools

_____ Prepare to ask for referrals

_____ Consider anticipated next steps

☛ READY, AIM, FIRE!

Build Your Own Pre-Call Planning Checklist

Take a few minutes to develop your own custom pre-call planning checklist. Think about what you need to do before every sales call, whether it will be on the phone or in person. Remember to include the 10 key issues on pages 46 and 47.

✓

_____ _____

_____ _____

————— ——————————————————————————————

————— ——————————————————————————————

————— ——————————————————————————————

————— ——————————————————————————————

————— ——————————————————————————————

————— ——————————————————————————————

————— ——————————————————————————————

————— ——————————————————————————————

————— ——————————————————————————————

————— ——————————————————————————————

Click Here!

If you want to print out the forms for free you can go to our web site at www.silverbulletselling.com.

Pre-Call Planning Tips

1. Working without a plan is the same as navigating without a map. It increases the amount of time and effort needed to reach your desired destination.

2. The best time to plan is before you go into battle. No matter how busy you are, take time at the beginning of the day or before each sales call to do some pre-call planning.

3. Develop a pre-call planning checklist with a colleague. You'll enjoy the process and come up with a better, more comprehensive checklist.

4. Use your pre-call planning checklist before every sales call.

5. Revise your pre-call planning checklist to keep it up to date.

6. Share your pre-call planning checklist with colleagues so they can improve their performance and make more sales.

7. Use pre-call planning to differentiate yourself from the competition.

8. People do not plan to fail, they fail to plan.

9. Use pre-call planning to feel more confident on sales calls. When we feel prepared, our anxiety is reduced.

10. Following a predictable pre-call planning checklist will help us to create more predictable results.

STEP TWO

Building Rapport

1. Pre-Call Planning
2. **Building Rapport**
3. Discovery
4. Tailored Solution
5. Addressing Concerns
6. Closing the Sale

CHAPTER NINE

Building Rapport Overview

The secret to rapport is getting to know the people you're selling to. They need to be convinced you have their best interest at heart.

—G.A. Bartick

Building Rapport Defined

Q: What does it mean to build rapport?

A: "Rapport" refers to the relationship or bond that develops between you and your buyer. The building blocks of rapport are the way you interact and communicate with others.

Q: Why is building rapport so important?

A: Our success in business (and in life) often depends on how well people like and trust us. Fortunately, we can learn techniques that help us interact and communicate more effectively, which will lead to more trusting, rewarding relationships.

So far you've completed your pre-call planning. Among other things on your pre-call planning checklist, you've researched your buyer online, MapQuested directions to the office (and if you're obsessive like me, you've done a dry run the night before), put an agenda together for the meeting (more on this in Chapter 10), practiced your credibility statement (see

Chapter 11), created a list of discovery questions (see Chapter 15) you want to ask, and addressed the 10 key issues of pre-call planning.

Could You Be Better . . .

At building rapport?

Could you be better at . . .

Y N Making a stellar first impression with your buyers every time?

Y N Consistently impressing your buyers with your professionalism, organization, and efficiency?

Y N Developing more trusting relationships?

Y N Building strong relationships with people you like, admire, and appreciate?

Y N Transitioning from preliminary pleasantries into the business conversation at the beginning of a meeting?

Y N Establishing your credibility?

Y N Speaking in terms of your buyers' interests and needs?

Y N Creating a unique and different buying experience for your buyers?

Y N Developing business partnerships with your buyers? (You know you're good when they start asking your advice on issues that do not relate to your product or service.)

A Bullet from G.A.'s Chamber

No one would argue that building a little rapport with a buyer at the beginning of a meeting is a great way to get things started. However, research tells us that people have different ideas about the best way to go about doing it. During my days as an insurance broker, I learned my lessons the hard way.

I had an initial face-to-face meeting with a prospect, the CFO of a posh law firm who was looking for some additional life and disability insurance. I did my pre-call planning by researching the firm on the Internet and checked in with his receptionist at 10:50 for an 11:00 meeting. At 11:00, the CFO's assistant escorted me into the office. On the wall was a picture of a foursome on the first tee at Pebble Beach, with the CFO standing right in the middle. I immediately jumped into a discourse about handicaps, courses, and who was going to be fitted for this year's green jacket. Mr. CFO perked up right away and engaged in a lively conversation. This went on for a good 15 minutes and I thought, "Wow! This meeting is off to a great start." When I noticed him glance at his watch, I politely asked how he was doing for time. Beads of sweat began to form on my upper lip as he told me he had a conference call at 11:30. I spent the next 15 minutes trying to squeeze in a 25-minute sales presentation. I blew it. I knew it. And I knew he knew it when I didn't get invited back.

Now you're ready to move on to Step 2 of the Bullet Selling process. It's time to develop a little rapport with your buyers when you meet face-to-face or on the phone. Realize that finding some common ground is important, but it's not the most important part of building rapport.

Let's take a minute to think what rapport is really all about. Think of a relationship you have right now with someone you like, respect, appreciate, and trust. It doesn't matter if it's a business or a personal relationship, as long as it is resilient and you have each other's best interest at heart. It's a relationship that amplifies your strengths and makes you a better person. Imagine what it would feel like if you were able to build these mutually beneficial relationships, based on trust and appreciation, with most of your buyers. How awesome would that be?

$500 Sales Tip!

One of the secrets to building credibility and integrity is to under-promise and over-deliver.

—G.A. Bartick

How do you go about developing such relationships? Fulfilling relationships are built from three elements:

1. Credibility
2. Integrity
3. Dependability

"Credibility" simply means that you've earned the right. You build credibility by letting buyers know you have the experience necessary to do the job exceedingly well.

"Integrity" means being honest and truthful in all of your interactions. You build integrity by being honest, especially when the truth is not necessarily to your advantage.

"Dependability" means that you are reliable over an extended period of time. You build dependability by repeatedly doing what you say you're going to do.

Rapport is the key to developing all three of these elements. As I said, rapport is the relationship or bond that develops between you and your buyer. It doesn't matter if you work in retail, where you may interact with a buyer only once, or if you work in a profession where you develop your relationship over many months or years; building rapport has to happen quickly. The Bullet Selling process allows you to build credibility, integrity, and dependability, whether you sell in an immediate or long-term sales cycle. You can build rapport in both a long-term process and a one-time meeting.

Building rapport begins little by little and day by day. Think of every interaction you have with a buyer as a building block. The goal is to make every one of these interactions positive. In other words, you want your buyers to leave the interaction feeling better than they did before. This is the essence of building rapport, and this is exactly what the Bullet Selling process is intended to do, and do quickly.

Building rapport quickly is what the next couple of chapters are all about. It will give you the tools you need to become a master of building rapport and creating a unique and different buying experience. The three rapport-building techniques we'll be working on in Chapters 10 and 11 are:

1. Preliminary pleasantries
2. Agenda statement
3. Credibility statement

CHAPTER TEN

Preliminary Pleasantries and the Agenda Statement

Preliminary Pleasantries Start the Ball Rolling

Does my misadventure with the golfing CFO sound familiar? Many people have the impression that talking about golf, the weather, kids, or last weekend is building rapport. And they're right...to a point. I consider all of this banter and chitchat preliminary pleasantries. Don't get me wrong; preliminary pleasantries are very important at the beginning of a meeting to get things rolling. They're necessary to warm up buyers before you get down to business. I always start any interaction with three to five minutes of preliminary pleasantries, but anything longer makes me nervous because I know I'm going to need all the time I can get to build credibility and trust, and to understand my buyer's unique situation and complete the next steps of the Bullet Selling process.

Did you know...

Thomas Jefferson frequently purchased bottles of Lafite Rothschild for his good friend President George Washington.

While discussing the fine bouquet of a 1982 Chateau Lafite Rothschild Bordeaux is all well and good, we need to move from the preliminary pleasantries into a business conversation within a few minutes of sitting down. Research shows that serious buyers want to talk about their business, their successes, and their issues; they do not want to spend too much time on trivial things. If I had started my meeting with the CFO with a few minutes of preliminary pleasantries and then quickly moved into the business conversation, I might have had an opportunity to play golf with him instead of just talking about golf in our one (and only) 30-minute meeting.

Transitioning to the Business Conversation

After a few minutes of preliminary pleasantries, it's time to transition into the business conversation. Of the thousands of sales professionals we've observed, very few know how to do this effectively. The Bullet Selling process makes the transition seamless by using an agenda statement. This 60 seconds of magic will build momentum and let buyers know you are prepared and professional, and have done this before.

The agenda statement establishes the purpose of the meeting, what you are going to cover, and how buyers will benefit from your time together. When they feel you are prepared and focused on helping them, they will relax and be more cooperative. In addition, the agenda statement removes one of the biggest fears people have: fear of the unknown.

Have you ever been in a meeting with a business owner or buyer who is a total Type A personality? You may wonder why they always need to be in control and run the meeting. Our research indicates that the answer is they're too afraid the meeting will be a huge waste of time if they don't run it. However, these Type A personalities have also told us that when they meet with someone who can run an effective meeting, they are more than happy to relinquish the reins. That's why it's so important to quickly demonstrate that you know how to run a meeting. The agenda statement is your secret formula. It sets the meeting up for success in the first four minutes, and it sets you apart from the competition.

The Agenda Statement

First, I'll introduce you to the four steps of the agenda statement, and then I'll break each step down so you can see how to develop your own customized statement. The four steps of the Bullet Selling agenda statement include:

1. Purpose
2. Outline
3. INput
4. Transition

Think of "POINT" (**P**urpose, **O**utline, **IN**put, **T**ransition) to remember the steps. Now we'll go into each step in depth.

Step 1: Purpose

State the purpose of the meeting in one sentence. Make sure your purpose statement stays very high level and does not go into the actual agenda items that will be discussed during the meeting. (This is a very common mistake.) You want your purpose to be short and crisp so that your buyer's ears perk up.

> **Good Example**
>
> *The purpose of this meeting is to give you an opportunity to learn a little bit about First Commercial Bank and myself, and for me to learn a little bit about you and your organization.*

The What and the Why

This example does a great job of quickly letting the buyer know what the meeting is about, which will help focus and set him at ease.

> Poor Example
>
> *The purpose of this meeting is for us to get to know each other a little better by talking about my past experiences with United National Bank, Sanwa Bank, and now with First Commercial Bank and how my clients love working with me. Then we can talk about your current situation and how First Commercial Bank can help you reach your goals.*

The What and the Why

This example starts off well, but then the sales professional gets into some specific agenda topics (i.e., his banking background) that are more effective if they are discussed a little later in the meeting. This agenda statement is too "salesy," which would increase the buyer's resistance.

Step 2: Outline

The goal of the outline is to quickly identify the topics to be covered during the meeting. If you made the mistake of talking about them in your introduction, then you'll be repeating yourself and that's not a good thing. Make sure the outline is not too detailed and do not start discussing the topics until you have covered the entire outline (another very common mistake). Otherwise you'll detract from the momentum you are building.

During a first meeting with a buyer, there are six key topics to discuss:

1. Overview of company and myself
2. Buyer's current situation
3. Buyer's desired situation
4. Buyer's expectations of a product or company like yours
5. See if there is a good fit
6. Possible next steps

Good Example

...In order to make the best use of our time, I've put together a short agenda.

- *First, I'd like to start off by giving you a **brief overview of First Commercial Bank and myself.***
- *Then I'd like to ask you a few questions to learn about your **current situation.***
- *After that, we can discuss your **desired situation**; you know, where you see yourself and your company in the next couple of years.*
- *Next, I would really like to understand your **expectations** of a banker.*
- *And finally, if we feel there's a **good fit**, we can talk about some possible **next steps.***

The What and the Why

The good example quickly and clearly communicates the topics to be covered during the meeting. It will help your buyer see you as organized and efficient. More importantly, your agenda statement will help him relax because it has removed the fear of the unknown. Everything to be discussed has been communicated up front.

Poor Example

...To save time and keep us on track, I've put together this little agenda.

- *First, I'll tell you a little about me and First Commercial Bank. I'll let you know about the bank's history and my 13 years of experience as a relationship manager.*
- *Then, you can tell me about your current situation. It'd be great if you talked about what banking products you are currently using.*
- *Next, I'd like to talk about your desired situation. You know, where you'd like to see your business in two to three years and what products you believe you will need. And what I can do to help you get there.*
- *And finally, I'd like to understand your expectations of me. Things like how often you like to hear from me and how you like to communicate, whether by e-mail or phone call. I'll even give you my cell phone number.*
- *If, at the end, you feel First Commercial Bank is the bank for you, I'll show you how easy it is to switch.*

The What and the Why

This poor example is too detailed. The sales professional is going to be repeating himself when he starts to cover each agenda topic. Also, notice the third bullet point dealing with the desired situation. This sales professional is assuming the sale and putting himself in the role of the buyer's banker. This, no doubt, will increase the buyer's resistance.

Step 3: Input

We ask if there is "anything else" the buyer wants to cover. If the buyer gives an additional agenda item, we write it down, assure him we'll cover it, and then ask again if there is anything else he wants to cover. We repeat this process until the buyer says "no."

Good Example

Sales Professional:
> *Is there anything else you'd like to cover or discuss?*

Buyer:
> *Yes, in fact. I'd like to discuss your fees.*

Sales Professional:
> *Great, I'll write that down and we'll definitely discuss our fees. Is there anything else you have on your mind?*

Buyer:
> *Nope, that's it.*

The What and the Why

From our research we know that during meetings buyers often have thoughts and concerns on their mind that distract them from fully focusing on what the sales professional is saying. What if the buyer has an urgent and important topic to discuss? Can that become agenda item #1? *Yes it can!* Remember process, not script. Bullet Selling is a flexible process that allows you to adjust on the fly. If you move something into agenda item #1 because you feel it needs to be discussed first, you are still following the process.

If the buyer has the opportunity to mention any additional topics, he'll be more at ease and able to focus his attention on you. So always ask that input question, and keep asking until the buyer says something like "No, I have nothing else I want to discuss."

Step 4: Transition

During the transition you simply ask for permission to proceed to agenda item #1.

> ### Good Example
>
> *Then to get started, is it okay with you if I give a brief overview of First Commercial Bank and myself?*
>
> **(Wait for a "yes.")**

The What and the Why

The transition lets the buyer know you're done setting up the meeting and are ready to begin discussing the agenda topics. If you ask their permission to proceed, you'll give the buyer the sense that they are in control of the conversation, which will allow them to relax, lower their resistance, and open them up to what you have to say.

The key to being effective at communicating the agenda statement is to remember the steps and not try to memorize it word for word. Go ahead and take a few moments to memorize the steps of the agenda statement. Remember: POINT!

1. Purpose
2. Outline
   a. Company and myself
   b. Current situation

     c. Desired situation

     d. Expectations

     e. Fit

     f. Next steps

   3. INput

   4. Transition

The Agenda Statement in Third Person

The agenda statement creates a unique and different buying experience for your buyer from the get-go. How refreshing it is for them to be dealing with an organized sales professional who demonstrates he knows how to run an effective meeting. The agenda statement is the way to transition from preliminary pleasantries into the business conversation and build some credibility and rapport at the beginning of every business meeting or phone call.

$500 Sales Tip!

Don't memorize the words.
Memorize the process.
—G.A. Bartick

A major point to remember is to keep the agenda statement in the third person. For example, if you're a banker, talk in terms of "expectations of a banker," not "your expectations of me." Why? Because you are not the buyer's banker. You have not, to this point, earned the right to call yourself his banker. If you assume and start to use that type of language this early in the meeting, the wall of resistance will go up.

Why? Because people are afraid they are going to be 'sold.' Keep it in the third person, reduce their resistance, and increase their receptivity to your message.

I'm sure some of you are thinking "I've been taught over the years that you need to assume the sale!" All I can say is try using the agenda statement and keep it in the third person. You are only four minutes into the meeting; you'll have plenty of opportunity to assume the sale later. Now is just not the time.

The "Why" Behind the What and the Why

I know from our research that sales professionals are much more likely to change their behavior if they understand what I'm asking them to change and the reason behind it. I want you to understand the nuances of the Bullet Selling process, so throughout the book I will explain "the what and the why" behind many of the skills of Bullet Selling.

Likewise, the more your buyers know about what you're doing and why you're doing it, the more their resistance will drop. They will respond better to your recommendations if you provide them with the rationale behind your method.

Example: Putting It All Together

Here's an example of a complete agenda statement that a commercial banker would use with a new buyer during their initial meeting. Realize where we are in the meeting. You have sat down. You have done two to three minutes of preliminary pleasantries. Now it is time to transition into the business conversation. It may sound something like this:

Purpose: State the Purpose of the Meeting

Sam, I want to thank you for taking the time to talk with me this morning. The purpose of this call is to give us an opportunity to learn a little about each other.

Outline: Briefly Outline What You Will Cover

…In order to make the best use of our time, I've put together a short agenda.

- *First, I'd like to start off by giving you a brief **overview of First Commercial Bank and myself.***
- *Then I'd like to ask you a few questions to learn about your **current situation.***
- *After that we can discuss your **desired situation**; you know, where you see yourself and your company in the next three to five years.*
- *Next, I would really like to understand your **expectations** of a banker.*
- *And finally, if we feel there's a **good fit**, we can talk about some possible **next steps.***

INput: Gain Buyer's Input on Agenda

Sales Professional:
 Is there anything else you'd like to cover or discuss?

Buyer:
 Yes, in fact. I want to know about your fees.

Sales Professional:
 Great, I'll write that down and we'll definitely discuss our fees. Is there anything else you have on your mind?

Buyer:
 Nope, that's it.

Transition: Transition into Agenda Item #1

Sales Professional:
 Then, to get started, is it okay with you if I give a brief overview of myself and First Commercial Bank?

Customer:
 Go right ahead.

The Agenda Statement in a Nutshell

Bullet Selling is all about memorizing the process, not the actual words. Remember POINT:

1. **P**urpose
2. **O**utline
   a. Company and myself
   b. Current situation
   c. Desired situation
   d. Expectations
   e. Fit
   f. Next steps
3. **IN**put

   Is there anything else?
4. **T**ransition

   Wait for a "yes."

Demonstration

We have posted several audio files of agenda statement examples from different industries on our web site, www.silverbulletselling.com.

Build Your Own Agenda Statement

Spend a few moments developing your own agenda statement. Think of an upcoming business meeting and prepare an agenda statement you'll use to transition from preliminary pleasantries into the business conversation. Go ahead and write your responses on another sheet of paper or use the template at www.silverbulletselling.com.

Step 1. Purpose

_____

_____

_____

_____

Step 2. Outline

_____

_____

_____

_____

_____

Step 3. INput

_____

Step 4. Transition

_____

(Wait for a "yes"!)

☛ **READY, AIM, FIRE!**

Practice Delivering Your Own Agenda Statement

Top performers don't wing it. They practice and practice their communication skills out loud because they know sales is a verbal sport.

1. Read your agenda statement aloud twice verbatim, including the steps of the process. It might sound like this:

    "**Step 1.** Purpose: Sue, I want to thank you for taking the time to meet with me this afternoon. The purpose of this meeting is to give us an opportunity to learn a little about each other.

    Step 2. Outline: In order to accomplish this . . ."

    I know it sounds funny saying the names of the steps out loud, but doing so will help you memorize the process.

2. Read your agenda statement four to six times slowly until you begin to memorize the process (not the words, but the steps of the process).

3. Practice saying your agenda statement until you have the process memorized and can communicate it without your notes.

4. Take a break.

5. Repeat steps 3 and 4 until your delivery is smooth and uncanned.

6. Using a tape recorder, record your delivery to hear what you sound like. Assess what you hear and adjust your delivery until you are very satisfied. Make sure your tone of voice is enthusiastic, not monotone.

If you want feedback on the delivery of your agenda statement, send an audio file in an e-mail to me at ga@silverbulletselling.com. I'll listen to your delivery and send you back detailed coaching notes at no cost to you.

Begin Every Meeting with an Agenda Statement

Most effective businesspeople make very quick judgments, and a well-executed agenda statement creates a fantastic first impression. Remember: You don't get a second chance to create a fantastic first impression.

Let's review the formula one more time. After a few minutes of preliminary pleasantries, we make a transition to a business conversation (the reason we are there in the first place) by using an agenda statement, which outlines the meeting. Again, the four steps are:

1. Purpose
2. Outline
3. INput
4. Transition

At the end of transition, we get agreement from our buyer and proceed to our first agenda item. Sound simple enough?

Should every sales meeting begin with an agenda? Yes! What about when we are meeting a buyer for the third, fourth, or twentieth time? It's still the same. The only thing that changes is the purpose and outline.

You'll be amazed how much of an impact this simple technique will have on your meetings and sales appointments. In fact, this is the way you should start virtually every business meeting or conference call you have. What's amazing is that very few do. And that's great for you. By using the agenda statement up front, you will clearly differentiate yourself from your competition.

Serving Up a Million-Dollar Loan at Mickey D's

When I first learned the agenda statement, I was a mortgage broker. (Remember me, the broke broker?) I had been working for Rancho Coastal Funding for about eight months when Paul Butler, a top-producing Realtor in Del Mar, called and told me he had just sold a home for $1.4 million and that I was to call his client to help arrange financing for a $1 million loan. Paul also told me that his client, Mr. Jackson, already had a "banking relationship" but had agreed to talk with me.

I was about to dial Mr. Jackson's number when I realized how much I needed this loan and the money it would put in my bank account. So I put the receiver back down and decided to actually follow my process and do a little pre-call planning. I addressed the 10 key issues, and I even jotted down some notes for my agenda. I decided that the goal for the phone call was to close for an appointment.

I rehearsed my agenda statement several times and took a quick walk around the block to ease my nerves. Man, I needed this loan! Finally I stepped back into the office, took a deep breath, picked up the receiver, and dialed Mr. Jackson. I almost hung up the phone when I heard, "Hello, Ralph Jackson here."

"Hello, Mr. Jackson. This is G.A. Bartick over at Rancho Coastal Funding. Paul Butler asked me to give you a call. Congratulations on the purchase of your new home."

"Thanks."

"Ralph, the purpose of this call is to give you an opportunity to learn a little bit about Rancho Coastal Funding and myself, and for me to get to know you a little bit better to see if we can get you the best loan at the best rate possible."

"That sounds fine, G.A., but as I told Paul, I already have a banking relationship."

"That is not a problem at all. It's probably a good idea to talk with a few brokers to make sure you get the best loan possible. In order to help you with that, I would love to get together, show you what we do, and ask a few questions to see if I can possibly provide you with a better loan. If you like, I would be happy to come to your office or home. Or if you prefer, you can come down to my office."

"G.A., I'd rather meet at a neutral location. How about the McDonald's on Del Mar Heights Road?" Since my goal was simply to set the appointment, I agreed on meeting at the "neutral location."

Before the meeting, I actually typed up and printed two copies of my agenda—one for him and one for me. Why two copies? Because I knew I was going to be nervous and I did not want to forget anything. I needed the cheat sheet. I ironed my briefcase, made sure I had all the appropriate forms and collateral, and left 15 minutes early for the 5-minute drive.

When I arrived, Mr. Jackson was already there waiting for me. We took a seat and I reached into my briefcase and pulled out the two agendas. I handed him one, wiped the sweat off my upper lip, and launched into my agenda statement for the first time with a real buyer. Because the printed agenda was bullet pointed, I had to make it come to life. I executed the agenda statement perfectly. I stated the purpose and went through the outline. When I asked the input question, Mr. Jackson said, "G.A., I just want to make sure I get the best loan at the best rate and fees possible."

"Great. We will definitely make sure you have several options and are able to get the best loan for your situation. Let me note that. In addition to that, is there anything else you want to make sure we discuss?"

"No, I think you covered it."

"Well then, if it's all right with you, may I give you a brief overview of Rancho Coastal Funding and myself?"

To this day, I cannot explain exactly what happened next. Right then and there Mr. Jackson reached down into his briefcase and said, "Well, G.A., you have obviously done this before. Here are all my financial statements. If you take them and fill out the paperwork, I can stop on by tomorrow to sign them."

I thought to myself, "Did that just happen?" In a 10-minute meeting I got a $1 million loan all because of my agenda statement. From that moment I was a total believer.

Passion Is Contagious

Agenda statements, and every other communication tool for that matter, should be delivered with passion. Is enthusiasm the same as passion? Think about it. Can you fake enthusiasm? Yes, you can, and I believe people can see right through it. Fake enthusiasm raises what I call the "cheese factor," and nobody wants to buy from a cheesy salesperson.

Blast from the Past!

If you're not fired with enthusiasm, then
you'll be fired with enthusiasm!
—Vince Lombardi

But passion? Passion comes from the heart and cannot be faked. In fact, passion generates true enthusiasm. Here's some food for thought: What do gunpowder and passion have in common? Give up? They both provide the power to drive things forward.

Think about it. In the chamber of a firearm, gunpowder is ignited when the charge is struck with the hammer, unleashing the power to drive a bullet. In very much the same way, passion drives us forward in our business, in our relationships, and in our lives.

As a case in point, think about the people you know who have accomplished great things. Chances are they all share a passionate, enthusiastic zeal for what they do. Think of passion as the power cell for success.

Do not confuse passion with excitement, though. Excitement is that heart palpitation you feel at the stadium after seeing a bottom-of-the-ninth walk-off homerun, or how you feel just after the buyer says yes. But passion is that inner drive you feel when you are motivated to become a better ball player or sales professional. True passion is excitement supercharged with inspiration, motivation, and determination.

Blast from the Past!

Enthusiasm is one of the most powerful engines of success. When you do a thing, put your whole soul into it. Stamp it with your own personality. Nothing great was ever achieved without enthusiasm.

—Ralph Waldo Emerson

Passion is powerful stuff for the physical body too. Tests show that passionate people have lower blood pressure and resting heart rates, and they tend to be happier, healthier, and feel more fulfilled. They also have more life energy and mojo. Fortunately, passion and enthusiasm are contagious; they tend to rub off on people.

If passion and enthusiasm are contagious, though, then apathy and lethargy are contagious as well. You have to ask yourself, "What are people catching from me?"

CHAPTER ELEVEN

Building Rapport by Playing the Credibility Card

Some call it the elevator speech. Some call it the personal introduction. The Bullet Selling process calls it the credibility statement. No matter what you call it, when it's done well it establishes credibility, builds positive rapport, reduces resistance, and opens doors to new opportunities.

In business, the credibility statement is as essential as a business card. You need to be able to say who you are, what you do, and how people can benefit from you and your product, all in as little as 90 seconds. Most sales professionals are not very good at introducing themselves and communicating what they do. The standard answer goes something like this: "I'm G.A. Bartick, and I'm a Partner at OutSell." What does this introduction tell a buyer about G.A. Bartick? Not much. It does nothing to knock down the walls of resistance or build credibility.

Did You Know...

"Elevator speech" is a term taken from the early days of the dot-com boom when web development companies needed venture capital. Finance firms were so swamped with applications for money that they often awarded funding to those companies that could effectively articulate their business proposition within the span of a typical elevator ride.

$500 Sales Tip!

All buyers think their situation is unique
and different, but they want to also know
you have done this before.

—G.A. Bartick

As we discussed in Chapter 10, the agenda statement is a great way to transition into the business conversation with buyers. When you follow your agenda statement with a concise and crisp credibility statement, it's like delivering a 1-2 punch to the way your buyers position you in their minds. Remember, how you are perceived often determines how you are treated and how open buyers will be with you regarding their situation. The credibility statement is the second bullet in your chamber to lower buying resistance and communicate that you are a competent and successful professional.

Positive Effects of a Credibility Statement

- It will position you as a unique and highly competent expert.
- It will communicate how buyers benefit from your product or service.
- It will convey the value you bring to your buyers.

I have heard all sorts of introductions during my rounds with sales professionals. I've seen top performers use the 90-second credibility statement to introduce themselves just after the agenda statement with great success. By contrast, I've also seen less successful sales professionals wait until the end of the sales call to talk about themselves, their company, and their products. When asked to explain, they often say, "I was taught to talk about the buyer first before talking about myself." In the field, providing a credibility statement before launching into discovery seems to create an environment where buyers feel more comfortable being open and truthful with their responses. Buyers tell us that sales professionals who give them a quick overview of who they are, what they do, and how they do it generates much more credibility and trust.

Three Questions on Every Buyer's Mind

Buyers by nature are very self-centric. During their interactions with a sales professional they are asking themselves three questions:

1. Who are you?
2. What do you do?
3. What's in it for me?

The credibility statement is specifically designed to address these questions quickly and succinctly. It lets your buyer know you've helped buyers like them before and how they might also benefit from working with you. The credibility statement has four steps:

1. Your company and you
2. Typical buyer
3. Success story
4. Transition to discovery

Step 1: Your Company and You

We open the credibility statement with a short overview of your company and yourself. When I say overview, I mean five or six bullet points that speak to:

- Your company's history
- Your company's niche or area of specialization
- Two or three features about your company
- Your relevant experience

Below is an example of a credibility statement that a sales professional from a bank might use when first meeting a buyer. Remember where we are in the process: The banker has sat down with the buyer and engaged in some preliminary pleasantries, transitioned into the business conversation with his agenda statement, and now is about five to six minutes into the meeting. The time has come for him to communicate who he is and what he does and, most importantly, to show that he is an expert and has helped similar buyers before.

> **Good Example: Your Company and You**
>
> *Michael, I'm not sure how much you know about First Commercial Bank. It was founded in 1973. With over $9 billion in assets, our clients know us as a bank that is small enough to provide individualized attention, yet big enough to offer a sophisticated line of products and services such as foreign exchange, wealth management, cash management, and international products. I have been in banking for nine years and came over to First Commercial three years ago because I really value the customer focus we have here.*

The What and the Why

This example does a fine job of positioning the sales professional as a banking expert and the bank as full service and buyer-focused. Just like that, the banker has addressed two of the three questions on every buyer's mind: who are you and what do you do. Upon hearing this, most buyers will realize they are working with someone who is credible and deserves respect.

Step 2: Typical Buyer

Follow up your company and you with a description of your typical buyer. Your description should resemble the buyer you are speaking to. Doing so will build credibility because it will give your buyer confidence that you have worked with buyers like him before.

> **Example: Typical Customer**
>
> *My typical customers are small businesses such as dry cleaners, manufacturers, and small law firms that are looking for additional capital to grow their businesses.*

The What and the Why

Buyers don't like it when they're the guinea pigs. That's why we customize this part of the credibility statement to describe the buyer we are talking to. Doing this allows you to show your expertise in their type of business. If you can use the names of other buyers you work with, all the better. (In some industries, such as financial services, you are not allowed to name your buyers for security and confidentiality reasons.)

Step 3: Success Story

During your credibility statement, share a success story that illustrates how one of your buyers has benefited from working with you.

There are three parts to telling a compelling success story:

1. Issue

   Describe the issue your buyer had.

2. Resolution

   Explain how you helped your buyer resolve the issue.

3. Benefit

   Explain briefly how your buyer benefited from the resolution and "dollarize" it if you can. This means letting the person you are talking to know how much money your service or product made or saved your buyer.

Example: Success Story

As a matter of fact, I am working right now with an owner of a chain of dry cleaners.

(ISSUE:) He wanted to purchase two more dry cleaners and buy some new equipment for his plant.

(RESOLUTION:) I put together an $800,000 line of credit that he used to purchase the two new locations and a $250,000 equipment lease for a new Forenta system.

(BENEFIT:) By doing so, he has added an additional $465,000 of profit annually to his company.

The What and the Why

A well-told success story builds your credibility by illustrating that you've helped other buyers in similar situations. In fact, our research indicates that likability and credibility increase significantly when a buyer hears about the success others have had working with you. So if you sell to several different industries, it will be important to develop different success stories for each industry.

Fact or Fiction

Before we jump into the fourth and final step of the credibility statement, I want to share a quick word about facts versus opinions. When talking with buyers, it is important that you speak in facts rather than opinions, especially early in the sales relationship. State facts that can be proven to be true and avoid making broad generalizations such as, "Our customer service is the best," or "Our product outperforms all others."

Opinions and generalizations in your credibility statement do not have the same impact as fact, and they will raise buyers' internal "I'm-being-sold-o-meter." So keep to the facts and let your competition talk in terms of opinions.

Step 4: Transition to Discovery

The last part of your credibility statement is transitioning into the Discovery step (i.e., Step 3 of the Bullet Selling process) by asking permission to ask questions. Like with the transition step in the agenda statement, wait for the buyer to say "yes" before moving on.

> **Example Transition**
>
> *So now that you know a little bit about First Commercial Bank, may I ask you a few questions so I can learn more about you and your company?*
>
>   (Wait for a "yes.")

Putting It All Together

Now that you know the four steps of the credibility statement, let's put it all together.

 Click Here!

To hear several examples of credibility statements from different industries, log on to www.silverbulletselling.com.

Introduction: Example Your Company and You

Mike and Jennifer, I would like to give you a brief overview of Cottonwood Realty and myself. Cottonwood Realty has been serving South Orange for over 25 years. We have 17 brokers and sold over $210 million in real estate last year.

I've been with Cottonwood for the past six years and last year I sold 19 homes in a down market with an average listing time of 27 days, when the rest of South Orange averaged 52 days. Currently I have six homes listed.

Typical Client: Describe Your Typical Client (*in this case a seller*)

My typical clients are sellers who are looking to work with an agent who has the experience to market their property, negotiate the deal, and close the sale quickly and efficiently.

Success Story: Illustrate How Your Customers Benefit

As a matter of fact, I was working with the Gilmans over on Crest Drive.

(ISSUE:) *Mrs. Gilman took a new job in Florida and so they needed to sell their home. It had been on the market for seven months prior to me listing their home.*

(RESOLUTION:) *I gave them some suggestions to help the home show better and put together a comprehensive and customized marketing program.*

(BENEFIT:) *We sold the home 2% below asking price and did it in 19 days.*

Transition: Transition to the Discovery Step with a Question

So now that you know a little more about Cottonwood Realty and myself, may I ask you a few questions to help me understand you and your situation better?

(Wait for a "yes.")

☛ READY, AIM, FIRE!

Build Your Own Credibility Statement

Now that you understand how the credibility statement works, it's time for you to customize it and try it yourself. The first thing you need to do is gather the ammunition you are going to use. On the lines provided or on a separate sheet of paper (you can also go to silverbulletselling.com for printable worksheets), write down the key points you may want to use in your credibility statement. Come up with as many points as you can to build your "reserve power." You need to have a lot of different facts, features, and success stories that you can pull from depending on the specific situation. I like to have a lot of ammo at the ready so I can choose which bullets I want to use with a particular buyer.

Build Your Own: Company

Write down eight to ten key facts about your company. Things like:

- When it was founded
- What the company specializes in
- Awards won
- Number of employees, assets, etc.
- _____
- _____
- _____
- _____
- _____
- _____
- _____
- _____
- _____
- _____

Build Your Own: You

Write down four to five key facts about you. Things like:

- How long you've been with the company
- How long you've been in the industry
- Why you like your company
- Any designations or licenses you may have (Series 7, Realtor, Certified Electrician)
- Any advanced degrees you may have

- _____
- _____
- _____
- _____
- _____
- _____

Build Your Own: Typical Buyers

Think about who your typical buyers are. You can call them by name, industry, or need (e.g., all my buyers want to improve the performance of their sales teams).

_____

_____

_____

_____

Build Your Own: Success Story Worksheet

It's important to have several success stories at the ready so you can interchange them to best fit the buyer you are speaking to. Let's spend a few minutes now building your library of success stories. You can also print this worksheet at www.silverbulletselling.com.

Buyer:

_____

Issue:

_____

_____

_____

Resolution:

_____

_____

_____

Benefit: (Dollarize it if possible)

_____

_____

_____

Build Your Own: Transition

Here's where you transition into the Discovery step with a question.

_____

_____

Putting It All Together

Now that you have developed and collected all the ammunition you need, it's time to make your own customized credibility statement. Think about a sales call you have coming up in the near future and rework your credibility statement for that meeting. Remember, a credibility statement should take about 90 seconds to deliver. Go ahead and write your credibility statement on a sheet of paper or download the form at silverbulletselling.com.

☛ READY, AIM, FIRE!

Practice Delivering Your Own Credibility Statement

Simply practicing in your head is not enough. Whenever I practice something in my head, believe me, it sounds so smooth and eloquent. But the words never come out of my mouth as well as they do in my mind. Does this ever happen to you? If you want your credibility statement to sound crisp and natural, then you have to practice it out loud. As with your agenda statement:

1. Read your credibility statement aloud four to six times slowly until you begin to memorize the process. Remember the four steps:
   a. Your company and you
   b. Typical buyer
   c. Success story
   d. Transition into Discovery
2. In the mirror look yourself in the eye while delivering your credibility statement. Use your notes if you have to.
3. Practice saying your credibility statement until you have memorized the 4 steps of the process.
4. Take a 30-minute break.
5. Repeat steps 3 and 4 until your delivery is smooth.

6. Using a tape recorder, record your delivery to hear what you sound like. Assess what you hear and adjust your delivery until you are very satisfied. Make sure your tone of voice is enthusiastic, not monotone.

If you want feedback on the delivery of your credibility statement, e-mail an audio file to me at ga@silverbulletselling.com.

Using the Credibility Statement

Obviously, you use the credibility statement when you are introducing yourself to a new buyer. However, the statement is just as important with established relationships. Every so often we want to update and build our image in our buyers' minds by reinforcing our credibility and value.

You can also use your credibility statement in situations like these:

- When someone asks you what you do for a living in casual conversation
- When describing what you do to family and friends
- On a plane at 30,000 feet chatting with the person sitting next to you
- At a chamber mixer
- At a cocktail party

Building Rapport Tips

1. Remember that curiosity, an open mind, a caring heart, and a genuine desire to help will enable you to build rapport with your buyer.
2. When talking with people for the first time, make a big deal out of getting their names right. They will appreciate it—trust me. To do so:
   a. Focus 100% concentration on the person you are meeting. Make sure you hear the name correctly. Ask for the correct pronunciation if necessary.

b. Use vivid visual pictures and name associations.

c. Repeat the name silently to yourself. Use the person's name in the conversation occasionally.

3. Listening is the gateway to building rapport. Effective sales professionals build rapport by listening for 70% of a conversation and speaking for only 30%.

4. Realize that all buyers prefer to do business with people they like and trust. Gain an edge on your competition by creating a unique and positive buying experience.

5. Take an interest in what the other person is saying. Be in less of a rush to talk about yourself. Listen to understand, not to respond.

6. Read Dale Carnegie's classic, *How to Win Friends and Influence People*. Then read it again.

7. In virtually every conversation where influence is the goal, be sure to start with questions before giving suggestions.

8. Write thank-you notes every night to the people you came in contact with that day. Let them know how much you care and appreciate their effort.

STEP THREE

Discovery

1. Pre-Call Planning
2. Building Rapport
3. **Discovery**
4. Tailored Solution
5. Addressing Concerns
6. Closing the Sale

CHAPTER TWELVE

Discovery Overview

Discovery is so much more than fact finding. When you do it right, discovery forges an emotional connection between the sales professional and the buyer, which sets you apart from the competition. Many times the sale is made right there in discovery.

—G.A. Bartick

Discovery Defined

Q: What does "discovery" mean?

A: "Discovery" refers to an exchange of information and emotion. Effective discovery is built on a questioning model that allows the buyer the opportunity to talk about their situation and the sales professional to actively listen and truly understand the buyer's situation before presenting any solutions. That's why effective discovery is equal parts observation and inspiration.

Q: Why is discovery so important?

A: Effective discovery creates the opportunity to close more sales because it provides an exchange of information and emotion needed to build a customized solution that satisfies both the buyer's logical and emotional needs. When done correctly, it gives the sales professional the opportunity to show the buyer an understanding of their unique situation.

Think of where we are in the process. You completed all pre-call planning and you're feeling confident and well prepared. You arrived at the buyer's office 15 minutes early and now you're in the meeting and have begun building positive rapport with your buyer through a few minutes of preliminary pleasantries. You have deftly moved into the business conversation with your agenda and credibility statements, and you have let your buyer know, in no uncertain terms, who your typical buyers are and how they benefit from working with you.

Right now, how is your buyer feeling and what is he thinking? If you've done a good job through the first two steps of the Bullet Selling process, then the buyer probably is feeling like he is talking to an experienced, competent sales professional. Even if you've done a stellar job up to now, though, your buyer's wall of resistance is still fairly high and his receptivity to what you have to say is still fairly low. The good news is that by your careful attention to details, you are earning the right to pursue the business conversation and transition into the Discovery step.

Remember, at the end of the credibility statement we transitioned into Discovery by asking the buyer for permission to ask him questions (*"If it is okay with you, may I ask you a few questions so I can learn a little bit more about you and your organization?"*), and we won't continue until the buyer gives us permission with a resounding "yes."

Discovery Is More than Fact Finding

Before we wade too deep into the discovery pool, let's think about the word "discovery" for a minute. What does it mean? According to *Webster's* (a sales book wouldn't be complete without at least one reference to the dictionary), "discovery" is "the act or process of discovering. To be the first to find out, see, or know about. To learn the existence of, realize. To reveal, disclose, expose or uncover." *Webster's* also provides a legal definition: "the methods used by parties to a civil or criminal action to obtain information held by the other party that is relevant to the action."

$500 Sales Tip!

During discovery, avoid the temptation to launch into a discussion of what you can do for your buyer. Save all that good advice for the tailored solution step.

—G.A. Bartick

I'm as unimpressed with that definition as you are. So let's dig a little deeper and see how Wikipedia defines the word.

> *Discovery observations form acts of detecting and learning something. Discovery observations are acts in which something is found and given a productive insight. Questioning is a major form of human thought and interpersonal communication, and plays a key role in discovery. Discoveries are acquired through questions.*

What do you think of these definitions? Personally, I think they're weak and pathetic because they talk about only half of the meaning of the word. They talk about the logical side and do a good job of describing "discovery" as an act of discovering through questions, but they completely disregard the emotional component of the word. The act of discovery gives rise to good feelings of gratification, delight, excitement, and appreciation. From observing thousands of sales calls, I have found there is a lot more to discovery than just asking questions and getting information. The process of discovery, when done correctly through the Bullet Selling process, culminates in what I call an "aha" experience for both the sales professional and the buyer. The aha for the sales professional is the excitement and delight that comes with the full understanding of the buyer's current and desired situations and their expectations (including both their emotional and logical needs). The aha for the buyer is the gratification and appreciation of being understood and listened to instead of being sold. Think about it. How good does it feel when someone takes the time to really listen to you and understand you and your situation? I don't know about you, but I think it is a pretty good feeling. And ever since I graduated from kindergarten, it just doesn't happen nearly often enough.

Discovery: Taking a Page from Columbo

Our research shows that most sales professionals under 35 years of age think Columbo is a yogurt. Think again (and get some culture). Peter Falk played Lieutenant Columbo from 1971 to 1978 and many regard him as the best television detective of all time. That's a pretty incredible claim considering the competition—Kojak, Baretta, Joe Friday, Starsky and Hutch, and my personal favorite, Magnum, PI. What made Columbo the *detective extraordinaire*? It wasn't his incredible criminal mind or his uncanny knack for getting people to confess to their crimes. It was the questions he asked. He had a penchant for asking just the right questions at just the right time. He understood that the right question would unlock the secret and solve the case.

Blast from the Past!
I know, it's because I keep asking these questions, but I'll tell ya', I can't help myself. It's a habit. Just one more thing …
—Columbo,
Murder by the Book, Episode 1,
September 15, 1971

In very much the same way, the right discovery questions unlock opportunities because they uncover the buyers' current situation, their desired situation; their wants, interests, and needs; and their expectations. And once we understand their unique situation, only then can we deliver a tailored solution that will satisfy them. Make sense?

Positive Effects of Good Discovery Questions

1. They help you uncover your buyer's wants, interests, and needs.
2. They help you truly understand each buyer's unique situation.
3. They engage your buyer in a conversation focused on him.
4. They lower buyer resistance and build receptivity.
5. They create a different and unique buying experience for your buyer.

As you talk to your buyer, it is important to use an effective sequence of questions that will gradually lower his resistance and build receptivity, allowing him to share sensitive information about his objectives, issues, risks, desires, and goals. You have to earn the right to ask some very personal questions. And remember, most people do not want to admit they do not know something or have not done something such as saving for their children's college education or planning for the future.

Listening to Understand versus Listening to Respond

Have you ever been talking to someone and, as you were talking, they were making sounds like "Uh, ooo, uh" and trying to jump in to talk at your slightest pause? How does that make you feel? What is that person saying with his actions? I think these people are saying "Shut up and let me speak, because what I have to say is more important than what you have to say!" When someone does that to me, I begin to get anxious and talk faster. Has this ever happened to you? Is this person listening to understand or listening to respond? The concept of listening to understand versus listening to respond may be the most important topic we cover in this book. It is an idea that, once you adopt it, will help you to reap benefits in your personal life as well as your business life.

$500 Sales Tip!

When conducting discovery, use active listening skills by nodding your head and using verbal prompts like "uh-huh" and "tell me more." If you have to, pretend you are hearing this for the very first time. Just listen. Do not judge!

—G.A. Bartick

Listening to understand is taking the time to comprehend and appreciate someone's situation. It's asking questions and then paying close attention to what the person is saying, then asking great follow-up questions to learn even more. It's important that you simply listen, understand, and not pass judgment. During discovery the buyer is doing most of the talking, answering our questions. Our research shows that most sales professionals listen to respond, not to understand, interrupting their buyers to present solutions. Listening to respond inhibits your ability to understand a buyer's unique situation, which will inhibit sales.

Could You Be Better. . .

At discovery?

Could you be better at . . .

Y N   Using a questioning model that helps lower your buyer's resistance and invites an honest exchange of information?

Y N   Forging an emotional connection with your buyer through your discovery process?

Y N   Listening to understand your buyer?

Y N   Taking great notes for an entire meeting on a single sheet of paper?

Y N   Building momentum and enthusiasm throughout the discovery process?

Y   N   Creating excitement, even if you sell boring products?

Y   N   Going through the entire Discovery process before launching into your sales
        pitch?

A Bullet from G.A.'s Chamber

We bought our house in San Diego in 2003. Actually, we bought a lot, and by the time we were finished with construction and all the upgrades we didn't have any money left for landscaping. So after about a year, my wife and I decided we were tired of watching tumbleweeds blow across our backyard and the kids playing in the dirt. The time had come for some landscaping. Neither of us knows much about gardens and plants, so we asked neighbors for referrals and looked in our local directory. We called one landscaper who had taken a big, bold ad in the directory and another who had placed a small, ordinary ad.

A few days later Big Bold pulled up in his fancy new truck with the name of his company glistening in gold letters across the side. He stepped out of the cab with a wide-brimmed cowboy hat on his head, a fat binder under his arm, and a smile across his face. He looked confident and successful and I was immediately at ease. I met him at the door and eagerly took him on a tour of the property.

Big Bold took one look around and I could tell he was not pleased. He asked me if the property had a sprinkler system. Of course the answer was no—my front yard looked like a desert. He asked if I had been seasoning the soil with fertilizer. Again, no. He then flipped through his fat binder, settled on a page, and showed it to me. As I was looking at the page, the landscaper explained, "These are some pictures of the backyard that's just right for you. I put this in for the Hodges' around the corner on La Plata Road. It's easy maintenance, it has a nice patch of grass and trees, and they love it. See the letter they wrote on the next page in the binder." While it was clear the Hodges' loved their backyard, I knew it was not right for me. First of all, half of it had been cemented to make a patio. My wife and I didn't want a patio. And where the patio ended, there was a nice field of green lush grass. But where was the herb garden we wanted and the fruit trees? As the discussion continued, I started to feel more and more uneasy because the landscaper didn't bother to ask what we wanted. He then launched into his sales pitch, went over costs, and pulled out his order form and asked me to put my John Hancock on it right then and there. I quickly retreated and had him leave the estimate and his card. Then I said good-bye, knowing that I'd never call him again.

I'd scheduled Small and Ordinary to meet us at the house about an hour later, and he pulled up in a well-weathered pickup. He stepped out of the cab with a baseball cap on his head, a pencil behind his ear, and a wire-bound notebook under his arm. The sight of Small and Ordinary did not instill much confidence in me. All the same, I met him at the front door and gave him the same 20-cent tour.

> ### Did you know...
> John Hancock was the only delegate to sign the Declaration of Independence on July 4, 1776. The other 55 delegates signed on August 2, 1776. Legend has it that Hancock signed his name in big bold letters so that King George III of England could read it without his spectacles, causing his name to become synonymous with "signature" ever since.

Small and Ordinary started to look around, and a smile came to his face. He then began to ask me a few questions. "Tell me what you're looking to do with your backyard."

"We want to plant a small herb garden," I replied.

"Really, why is that?"

"Kelly, my wife, is a gourmet cook (as I patted my well-developed midsection), and she's excited about cutting fresh herbs from her garden to season her feasts."

"What else would you like?"

"We'd also like some grass for the kids to play on, a dog run on the side, maybe some fruit trees, and, most importantly, a half-court basketball court. We want to convert this patch of dirt into our dream backyard! But we don't want to spend a lot of time or money maintaining it. That's really important."

"I understand," he said, nodding. "What kind of fruit trees do you have in mind for your orchard?"

"The kids love peaches and plums, and we were thinking we'd like a few trees of each."

I realized that I liked talking to this guy, and I was starting to feel a little more comfortable. Then he turned his attention to the grass. He asked me what we planned to do on the grass because that would dictate what kind of seed to plant.

"We want grass where our kids can roll around and play. It also has to stand up to the abuse doled out by three greyhounds. And I'm looking forward to Sunday afternoon naps on my bed of grass after playing on my half-court basketball court." The basketball court was the crown jewel, the pièce de résistance. The landscaper asked if I played and I shared that I had in high school. (I was the starting center on the 14–1 Foothill Knights, Century League Champions in 1983.)

Small and Ordinary then asked, "Can you tell me a little about what you are looking for in a landscaper?"

I had never thought of that so I took a moment before I told him, "We're looking to work with someone who listens to what we want and offers some good suggestions. We've never designed a backyard before, so we really don't know what the options are so we want to work with an experienced landscaper. We also need to work with someone who's fair and doesn't get frustrated if we change our minds. We're new to this and have to feel okay about changing direction. What's most important to us is working with a landscaper who will finish the job on time and on budget."

"I understand." Small and Ordinary smiled and asked me if I had any questions for him. Well, in fact, I did.

"Won't I need a sprinkler system?" The landscaper said it would probably be a good idea because we didn't want to spend a lot of time watering. I then sheepishly explained that the soil had not been seasoned with fertilizer and that it had lain fallow for more than a year. Small and Ordinary didn't think this was a particular problem; he would bring some topsoil to mix in.

The landscaper then summarized what he had learned. We wanted a low-maintenance backyard with an herb garden. We also wanted a small fruit orchard with several peach and plum trees and a field of grass (I loved when he said "field" even though he was only talking about our 100-square-foot plot) where the children and dogs could play and I could relax. And then he described the basketball court in vivid detail, complete with a painted key and regulation three-point line! He then explained my expectations of a landscaper. I wanted to work with someone with experience and who bid fairly on the project because I did not want to be nickel-and-dimed to death. And, most importantly, I wanted a landscaper that would finish the job on time. As he told me these things, I kept nodding, and a big smile stretched across my face. I was getting excited.

The landscaper then pulled the pencil from behind his ear and began sketching in his notebook. He sketched two different plans, each one satisfying our criteria. He then gave me a list of references from the area and invited me and my wife to drive around the neighborhood to see his work and talk to his clients after he left. He glanced over at my neighbors' yards and pointed out some other features from their landscapes that might interest me. After the consultation, Small and Ordinary left his card and we shook hands good-bye. The next afternoon my wife and I went around the neighborhood and talked to several of his clients who told us they were very happy with his work. We were getting more and more excited about the project and we called Small and Ordinary to ask for a proposal.

— — —

I knew we were going to hire Small and Ordinary the moment he left that day. However, when he first walked onto the property, I was a skeptic and my walls of resistance were high because of my experience with Big Bold. This is a *huge* point to understand. Creating that different buying experience is key because it gives you the advantage in a competitive buying situation. Also, you can't predict how buyers are going to react to you. Often it is heavily influenced by their previous experiences with other sales professionals. The fact is, the way your competition treats your buyers will impact the way your buyers respond to you.

Small and Ordinary got the job because he did such a phenomenal job of discovery. He asked some very good questions that gave him an understanding of our current situation, our desired situation, and our expectations of a landscaper. He obviously listened to me, based on his summary and the on-target sketches he drew. His discovery process lowered my resistance and increased my receptivity to his solution. This was important because his proposal was *more expensive* than Big Bold's. Through his sales process, Small and Ordinary had built additional value in his services that allowed me to make a positive buying decision to spend more money. That's what happens when you create a different and unique buying experience for your buyers.

CHAPTER THIRTEEN

The Goals of Discovery

The goals of the Discovery step are many and you need to understand each one in order to be most effective. In this chapter we are going to discuss these goals, including:

- Discovering the buying gap
- Lowering buying resistance
- Generating buying momentum
- Showing buyers that you are different from other sales professionals
- Learning buyer's current and desired situations and expectations

Discovering the Buying Gap

One of the goals of the Discovery step is to uncover the buyer's current situation and desired situation through a questioning flow I discuss in detail in Chapter 15. If the current situation and desired situation are sufficiently different, therein lies the buying gap. The buying gap is the difference between a buyer's current situation and desired situation.

Our research indicates that sales professionals waste a lot of time trying to sell to buyers who have a very small buying gap. If buyers have already reached their desired situation, it is going to be very difficult to convince them to purchase your product or service. I have seen many sales professionals spend countless hours writing proposals and working on deals that just aren't going to happen. That's why you need to ask good discovery questions: to assess the size of the buying gap and pursue only the leads where a significant buying gap exists. Let the other leads go and get them out of your pipeline so you can spend your valuable time and energy on buyers who need you and your product or service.

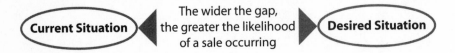

Current Situation — The wider the gap, the greater the likelihood of a sale occurring — Desired Situation

$500 Sales Tip!

Sometimes the buying gap is not evident to the buyer. That's your job, to bring it to their attention.

—G.A. Bartick

Listening Is the Gateway to Rapport

A well-executed Discovery step lowers buying resistance in two distinct ways. First, as people talk about themselves and what they want, they start to feel more comfortable and develop rapport with the person they're talking with. As rapport builds, resistance begins to fade.

Second, as we listen buyers begin to understand that we are taking a sincere interest in them and their situation. Listening is truly the gateway to rapport because it allows us to tap into the powerful principle of "seek first to understand before you seek to be understood" that was popularized by Stephen Covey in his best seller, *The 7 Habits of Highly Effective People*. The theory teaches that we become more effective in our relationships if we make it a high priority to understand others before we try to get them to understand us. When people feel understood, a sense of trust develops, reducing their resistance and increasing their receptivity.

How Experience Can Hurt Us

Often, when we conduct a Bullet Selling training program for a client, experienced sales professionals in the room announce at the beginning of the program that they have more than 15 years of sales experience, have taken every training program imaginable, and can't figure out why their company is putting them through the torture of yet another program.

"I have a ton of work to do. Why do I need to be here?" they grumble. However, when we observe these same experienced sales professionals in front of a buyer, we often find they are not very effective at discovery. In fact, new hires often outperform them at executing discovery. How can that be?

Veteran sales professionals tend to want to impress buyers with how much they know. They often take on the attitude of "I've heard your situation a thousand times. I know exactly what you need, so shut up and let me tell you what you need to know." When sales professionals cop this attitude they typically ask a few discovery questions then rush right into the solution. These professionals are so eager to show buyer's what they know that they do not take the time, or want to expend the energy, to learn about the buyer's situation.

Unfortunately, I've experienced this myself firsthand.

A few years after I started selling training and consulting services for OutSell, I knew our sales process inside and out. After several years of meeting with buyers week in and week out, I got to the point where I was able to intuitively tell what that buyer wanted and needed after about five minutes of discovery. And at least 90% of the time I was right. It's not rocket science. It was very tempting, especially when my patience was low, to abbreviate the Discovery step and questioning process and just tell buyers what they needed. I would say to myself, "Well, this situation is no different than what I've heard before. The Discovery step does not apply," and I would rationalize why I could skip a thorough discovery. It seemed more efficient because I could save about 30 minutes by not having to listen to what I had heard dozens of times before from other buyers.

The problem with doing this, as I began to find out, was that although the questioning process was very familiar to me, each buyer was going through it for the first time. What every buyer is going through during the discovery process is as important, if not more so, than what the sales professional is learning. By truncating the discovery process, I was compromising the rapport, trust, and momentum developing between me and the buyer, and in the end I was diminishing my effectiveness. Efficiency can get in the way of effectiveness and this is a trap that many experienced sales professionals fall into.

Discovery Generates Buying Momentum

The point I'm making here is that the Discovery step generates buying momentum, not just selling ammunition. Too many sales professionals look at discovery only as a fact-finding mission, where they need to gather the information they need in order to create a solution and make a sale. While this is true, it is only half the equation. The other half is forging that emotional connection with buyers we talked about earlier.

Something incredible happens when two human beings are really communicating with one another. An emotional bond is formed when a person feels safe enough to explain his situation to a person who is genuinely interested and concerned. People find it very satisfying to talk about themselves. During the Discovery step we want buyers to be thinking "This person really understands me and values what I have to say." When this happens, you are generating the positive emotions of enthusiasm and excitement, and building a relationship between you and your buyer.

$500 Sales Tip!

Customers don't care how much you know until they know how much you care.
—G.A. Bartick

CHAPTER FOURTEEN

Tools You Need to Accomplish the Goals of Discovery

O kay, now that you are armed with the goals of discovery, let's talk about how we're going to accomplish those goals. To be most effective, there are two things you need to know:

1. Buying criteria
2. Questioning flow

Buying Criteria

Buyers use three criteria when making decisions about what they want to purchase:

1. Buyer needs
2. Buyer wants
3. Buyer emotional criterion

To be truly effective, we need to be able to uncover all three of these criteria in our buyers before moving on to the Tailored Solution step.

Needs

When we talk about needs, we're referring to the factors that *must be satisfied* in order for buyers to make a positive buying decision. For instance, let's say that a buyer visits a Toyota dealer and tells the sales professional that he wants a vehicle that must have:

1. Room for four passengers
2. A large trunk
3. At least 25 miles per gallon
4. Satellite radio
5. A lease for under $375 per month

These five features would be considered the buyer's needs. These are the deal breakers, the must-haves, the features that must be in the solution in order for this buyer to move forward. Needs naturally vary from buyer to buyer; in fact, they may vary among members of a buying team. Sometimes the head decision maker has different needs from the people she has assembled to help her make the buying decision. One thing is for sure, though. If we do not satisfy the needs of the most important decision maker, we are very unlikely to win the sale.

Wants

Wants are the factors that we would like to have, if possible, but are not absolutely necessary. Wants are the added features that make the product/ service more appealing. For instance, staying with our car analogy, this buyer might want leather interior, a metallic burgundy paint job, and the increased power of the 3.5-liter, V-6 engine with 268 horses. If our buyer can get these wants in addition to his needs, then the deal becomes that much more appealing, or he may be willing to pay more for these features.

Fuzzy Wants Can Disturb that Delicate Balance

Sometimes sales professionals lose the sale because they focus more on satisfying the wants than on satisfying the needs. This is a pretty common mistake and it happens because sales professionals do not execute a thorough discovery and are not clear about which features are needs and which are wants.

Let's say the sales professional in our car analogy offers a Toyota Avalon and throws in the entire list of desirables plus:

- Top-of-the-line CD changer
- Sunroof
- GPS navigation system

And then when the nickels and dimes are all added up, the lease is up to $420 a month, which is $45 more than the buyer wanted to spend. The challenge for the sales professional is to help the buyer see the value for the wants and spend more. Certainly there are some buyers who will cough up the extra dough because they see the value and their desire for the wants is so high. But sometimes the extra charges will kill the sale.

$500 Sales Tip!

Think of discovery as the ladder that
will get you over the wall of resistance
and take you to the promised
land of success.

—G.A. Bartick

The Emotional Criterion

Needs and wants are "what" we want. The emotional criterion is "why" we want the product or service, and often it is the most important criterion of all. Remember, many times people buy to satisfy their emotions and then rationalize their purchase through logic.

Continuing with the car analogy, let's say the buyer decides to check out the competition over at the Mercedes dealer. The sales professional hears the same list of needs and wants, and offers the buyer a new C300 sedan with these features:

- Room for four passengers
- A medium-sized trunk
- 24 mpg highway
- Satellite radio
- Heated/cooled seats
- Sunroof
- Leather interior
- 228 horsepower V-6 engine
- A lease of $429 per month

Now the buyer starts to consider the emotional benefits of owning a Mercedes, including:

- The pride he'll feel when he takes it home and parks it in his driveway
- The points he'll earn from his wife and kids for bringing home a Mercedes
- The fun and excitement he'll feel every time he drives the car
- The way he and his wife will feel pulling up to a restaurant and handing the keys to the valet
- The satisfaction he'll feel when taking his work colleagues out to lunch
- The perception his clients will have of him when he pulls into their building for an appointment
- What his neighbors will say when he pulls up to the house

The buyer has a dilemma. The Toyota Avalon at $420 meets all of his needs and wants, but the Mercedes C300 satisfies his emotional criterion. If I were a betting man, I'd wager a lot of money that the buyer would buy the Mercedes.

Uncovering Buying Criteria

Now that we know what we're looking for—needs, wants, and emotional criteria—we need a method to uncover them. It would be great if we could simply ask, "What do you want most, what else do you want, and why do you want these things?" and then sit back and let our buyers pour it all out for us, but communication is much more subtle than this. People are sensitive and cautious about revealing too much about themselves, especially with people they have just met. In addition, most of us simply aren't aware of our buying criteria and we need a structured questioning flow to reveal them.

The Questioning Flow

The questioning flow begins with questions that are more general and gradually become more specific. It works best when we begin with general questions that are easy for buyers to answer.

For instance, let's say a very close friend you haven't seen in a while is coming to town. You go to the airport to pick him up and welcome him with a hug. What are you most likely to ask this dear friend? Do you start off by asking "So tell me, Andy, where do you see yourself two to three years from now?" That would be awkward. A better place to start is asking him about what's happening now—his current situation—because they are much easier questions to answer. Here are some examples:

- How's it going?
- How have you been?
- How is your family?
- What have you been up to lately?
- How are things at work?
- How are your kids?

When we rush into more personal questions too early, we will increase resistance and decrease rapport. Questions I would not ask during the first few minutes of the conversation would include:

- It's great to see you after so long. Tell me about your goals.
- How are you getting along with your wife?
- How are your finances?
- What problems are you facing in your life right now?
- How can I help fix your problems?

Although most of us don't make this kind of mistake in our personal lives, I have observed many sales professionals beginning the Discovery step with questions like these:

- What are your goals and objectives in the upcoming year?
- What are the work-related problems that keep you up at night?
- Tell me a little about your vision.
- How much have you saved for a down payment?
- How can I help you solve your problems?

Don't get me wrong, these are great questions to ask. It's just a bit early in the sales conversation to ask them, and buyers will most likely give us less thoughtful or less complete answers. In fact, often they will give us responses that throw us off the trail and lead us to a less effective solution. When faced with such intrusive questions, they feel like they're being sold and their resistance is even higher than it was at the beginning of the conversation.

In order to forge that emotional bond and uncover the logical information we need to generate a customized solution presentation, we need a questioning flow that satisfies both the emotional and logical components of the sales process. The flow is simple and, for most businesses, consists of these four pieces:

1. Current situation questions
2. Desired situation questions

3. Expectations of a sales professional and/or your product/service

4. Discovery summary

Current Situation Questions

The reason we start with the current situation is that people are typically more comfortable talking about things they know well. One of the keys to being a good conversationalist is to talk about things people know. As we open the conversation with questions, two things happen: (1) You learn about your buyers' situation, which helps you present a solution tailored to their circumstances, and (2) your buyers' resistance starts to drop, which will allow you to ask more delicate questions about their desired situation.

Desired Situation Questions

After we feel we have a thorough grasp of buyers' current situations, we then move into questions that shed light on their desired situations: what they want to see happen. Questions that probe into buyers' goals and desires are more difficult to answer for two reasons: (1) We are asking buyers to speculate and talk about things they may not have thought through entirely beforehand, and (2) the questions expose some of our buyers' shortcomings and issues.

As I mentioned, the sales opportunity exists in that gap between buyers' current and desired situations. We are looking for buyers who want something they don't already have, where our product or service can help them get it. The bigger the gap, the better.

Expectations of You and Your Product

These are some of the most important questions and the ones that are most often left out. We ask buyers about their expectations because it helps us understand what they are looking for in terms of working together. This is where we can ask questions about what they do or don't like about their current products, vendors, advisors, brokers, agents, and so on. We will use the information we gather during this line of questioning in our solution presentation.

We discuss current situation, desired situation, and expectation questions in detail in Chapter 15.

Discovery Summary

All of these questions set up the most important part of the Discovery step: the discovery summary. After we've gathered all of the information from the three lines of questioning, we deliver a compact, compelling, and accurate summary to our buyers. By presenting an on-target summary, you are showing your buyers that you have listened and are aligned with them. This is where the emotional connection between you and your buyers is forged. You'll know that your discovery summary is hitting the mark when you see your buyers nodding in agreement. In Chapter 16 we explore the content and delivery of the discovery summary.

CHAPTER FIFTEEN

You're Only as Smart as the Questions You Ask

I can hear some of you asking why I've given you all this background information about the Discovery step. Why couldn't I have just given you some questions to ask and be done with it? The answer has to do with the fact that this book is all about execution. There are many nuances when it comes to selling and for you to be able to execute the Bullet Selling process effectively, you need to understand why I am asking you to do certain things in certain ways.

In order to execute the Discovery step effectively, you need to be able to:

- Uncover the buying gap
- Lower buying resistance
- Generate buying momentum
- Deliver a powerful discovery summary

You can do all of this only if you understand your buyers' buying criteria through the four parts of the questioning flow you use (i.e., current situation questions, desired situation questions, expectation questions, discovery summary).

In this chapter we will present all four pieces of the discovery flow. Within the three questioning areas, the questions go from general to specific, starting with the most nonthreatening ones. Remember, this is the strategy we use to reduce resistance and build rapport.

As models, we are going to use actual questions that some of our clients in different industries use. In the examples, you'll notice that we list too many questions to ask during one discovery meeting. We do this to allow you to choose which questions you want to ask. You're in the business of building relationships and the expectation is that you will gather a great deal of information in your initial meeting and continue to add information during subsequent meetings. The key is to have what I call "Reserve Power," everything you need at your fingertips including agendas, credibility statements, and a complete battery of questions to ask at the ready. I'll tell you more about Reserve Power later in Part 3.

Asking Questions Is Not an Interrogation

There I was, minding my own business working with a systems networking sales professional. We were working on his discovery skills when he asked me, "Do your kids go to private school?" This seemed like an innocent enough question. I told him that no, my kids all go to public school. He looked up at me with his glasses perched at the end of his nose and subtly shook his head. I thought to myself, "Wow, I guess he thinks I can't afford private school." I found myself defending my decision to send my kids to public schools when I realized what I was doing and called a quick time-out. I asked why he asked me that question. He said that he works with a lot of private schools and he was hoping my kids went to a private school so that I might give him a good referral.

I was offended by the way he asked his question which sent my resistance level sky high. What other question could he have asked? How about "Where do your kids go to school?" That would have helped him get the same information. The questions you ask and the way you ask them are very important. You're not here to judge your buyers; you're here to learn about them and, during this stage of the process, what you say and *how* you say it are key. Be inquisitive, don't be judgmental.

It's Not about Pain

Many sales programs talk about creating pain or opening the wound and rubbing some salt in it as a way to sell. I believe that sales is not about creating pain, but about getting buyers excited about the possibilities and "seeing" their desired situation as an achievable reality. Our research shows this is a much more effective way to sell. And it is a much more enjoyable way to buy.

You know that buying creates fear and anxiety. Often people making the buying decision may literally be putting their jobs or security on the line by deciding to go with you. Help your buyers make a positive buying decision based on the vision of realizing their desired situation rather than bringing out the pain of what would happen if they were not to act and purchase your product or service.

Your job is to create the vision of possibilities for your buyer.

Pain Example

"Jack, I understand you want to bring in a new technology solution because your current systems are not talking to each other. And because of this, it is difficult to obtain good data, which causes your forecasts to be off. And because of this, you are missing some of the shipping dates to your clients. Is that correct?"

And the buyer says, "You're right, it's so frustrating!" as he shrinks into his chair.

Possibilities Example

"Jack, so if I understand correctly, you are looking for a company that can help your multiple computer systems talk to each other. If they were all talking to each other, then you would be able to obtain precise data. This would allow you to forecast accurately and your buyers would be able to more effectively and efficiently purchase supplies. And because of all of this, you'd be shipping products on time all the time. And if this happened, you believe it would create even more business and opportunities for you and the company. And that is what you really want, isn't it?"

And the buyer says, "Yes, that's exactly what we want!" as he reaches across and gives the sales professional a high five.

The differences between these two approaches are major, and so are the results. The pain solution gets the buyer slinking down in his chair as you create more and more pain. The person you are talking to may very well be the one who got the company in that situation in the first place. And with pain comes hesitation.

In the possibilities example, the buyer's head nods up and down as you articulate the desired situation in a way that is easy to picture and puts him in a place of excitement and receptivity.

The Importance of Taking Notes

We work with a lot of sales professionals who do not like to take notes during their sales calls. When we ask them to explain, they tell us their buyers would find it unprofessional. Others tell us something like, "I want to give my buyer my complete undivided attention. Taking notes is rude." I am writing this passage for all of you out there who share this belief. Remember, we have 11 filing cabinets full of notes from interviews with and observations of sales professionals and managers. Not once in any of these interviews and observations did anyone feel uncomfortable with note taking.

In fact, the opposite is often true. Decision makers prefer to work with sales professionals who write down all the important things they have to say. Buyers are flattered when you take notes. It shows them that you value what they are saying and that helps to build rapport. I don't know about you, but I love it when someone writes down what I say.

Another reason we need to take notes is that it prepares us for the discovery summary. All of the questions you ask are simply setting up this dramatic event in the sales process. Your discovery summary will be much more effective if you take good notes.

Understand that taking notes, asking questions, and knowing what to say next requires a lot of mental gymnastics and isn't easy. That's why it's so important to build that Reserve Power so you have the questions at the ready and you can simply sit back, listen to understand, and take brief notes.

How to Take Notes

During the Discovery step, buyers are going to share a lot of information with you. You want to capture the most important details in your notes so you will be more effective in summarizing the meeting and following up during your powerful discovery summary.

I used to take a ton of notes during meetings, only to go back to my office and have trouble deciphering them because of my sloppy handwriting and disorganization. I'd be asking myself, "What did I mean here?" or "What does that say?" or "Why did I put this comment here?"

My business coach, Mary Andrews (yes, I too have a coach), taught me the process of mind mapping and it has changed the way I take notes in everything I do. I have even taught it to my teenage daughter, Alicia, to use in school.

Mind mapping is a very effective note-taking technique. Mind maps are more compact than conventional notes, often taking up only one side of paper for an entire meeting. This makes them very quick to review. Also, conversations do not happen in linear fashion. When you're talking to a buyer, the conversation might skip from one topic to another and then back again. If you're taking conventional notes, they will be disorganized.

For example, let's say you're meeting with a buyer at a pharmaceutical lab and you start talking about the kinds of drugs your buyer manufactures. Then you move on to talking about purity concerns and, in the middle of this discussion, he remembers he left out the new diabetes drug going into production that he wants to tell you about. Unfortunately, you're already on your second page of notes, so you write this additional information about the diabetes drug on page 2, separate from the notes at the top of page 1 where it belongs.

Mind mapping is a great solution to this problem and you only have to use the process a few times to master it. What I like best about it is that I write half as much and get twice the information. I use it at meetings and to outline proposals and other business documents. At home, I mind map the planning of my Annual New Year's Day Brunch to celebrate my birthday. Basically, I mind map whenever I need to put pen to paper.

To make notes on a subject using a mind map, follow these five steps.

1. Write the title of the subject in the center of the page and draw a circle around it.
2. For the major subject subheadings, draw lines out from this circle. Label these lines with the subheadings.
3. If another level of information belongs to these subheadings, draw these additional lines and link them to the subheading lines.
4. For individual facts or ideas, draw lines out from the appropriate heading line and label them.
5. As you come across new information during the interview about a previously discussed topic, go ahead and link it to the mind map appropriately.

On the following page is a mind map of a meeting a pharmaceuticals sales professional had with a buyer.

$500 Sales Tip!

You can download (for a fee) your own mind mapping software at mindjet.com.

—G.A. Bartick

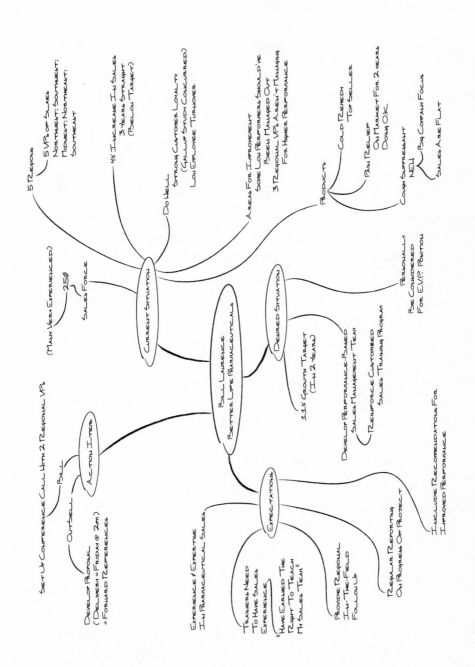

Discovery Question Flow Example

Industry: Marketing Business to Business

Before we look at our example call flow, I want to remind you how important it is to do your homework during your pre-call planning. Our research shows that buyers do not like answering questions they feel the sales professional should already know through industry experience or company research. In a 60-minute conversation, you want to spend your time asking questions that you can't find the answers to elsewhere.

We designed this questioning flow for a company that has a team of sales professionals selling marketing services to restaurant merchants. The questioning flow organizes its questions around six areas:

1. General information about their business: current situation
2. Marketing: current situation
3. Loyalty: current situation
4. General information about their business: desired situation
5. Marketing/Loyalty: desired situation
6. Expectations of a marketing partner

Current Situation: General Business
- How long have you been in business?
- How did you get involved in the restaurant business?
- How did you come up with this restaurant concept?
- What made you choose this location?
  - Is this your only location?
- Do you serve breakfast, lunch, and dinner?
- What are typically your slowest and busiest times?
- Who is your direct competition?
  - What would you say makes you different from your competition?
- What outside events affect your business the most?

Current Situation: Marketing

- What types of marketing/advertising are you using right now?
  - When and how often do you like to market?
- What has worked and not worked for you in the past?
  - What is the most effective thing you've done to promote your restaurant?
  - How do you know it worked?
- Have you tried to bring in restaurant customers from out of the area?
  - What types of results have you had?
  - How do you know?
- How do your customers typically find out about your restaurant?
- How do you determine the effectiveness of your marketing investments?
- How do you track your marketing results?

Current Situation: Loyalty

- Where do most of your customers come from?
- What would you consider to be a loyal customer?
- How often do your best customers visit your restaurant?
  - How do you know?
- What have you tried to get them to come back more often or spend more when they are here?
  - Has it worked?
  - How do you know?
- What do you think keeps customers coming back to your restaurant?
- How do you measure loyalty?

Desired Situation: General

- What plans do you have for your restaurant?
- Tell me about some of your goals or priorities.

- Where do you want to see your restaurant over the next couple of years?
- Do you plan on expanding?
  - Any other new projects?
- If you had extra capital available, what would you do with it? How would you like to improve your business?

Desired Situation: Marketing/Loyalty

- What are some of your marketing goals?
- Whom are you targeting?
  - What kind of customers are you looking to bring into the restaurant?
- Would you like to expand your reach to bring in more customers from outside the area?
  - If so, from where?
  - How would you know if this was working?
- How do you plan on attracting new customers or increasing frequency?
  - How will you know if your efforts are working?

Expectations of a Marketing Partner

- What are your expectations of a marketing partner?
- How do you like to work with your marketing partners?
- Tell me about your past relationships with other companies, advertisers, or marketing partners. What do you like about these relationships?
  - What did they do well?
  - What would you like to change?
- What is important to you in a relationship with people and companies you do business with?
  - Why?

Click Here!

For examples of questioning flows from other industries, visit our web site at silverbulletselling.com.

Follow-Up Questions

The questions in the questioning flow are called initial questions. We often follow up with clarifying questions.

Clarifying Questions

Clarifying questions typically ask buyers to be more specific or provide more information.

> *Example Clarifying Questions*
> - Can you tell me more about that?
> - What didn't you like about it?
> - What do you mean by that?
> - Can you help me understand that a little better?
> - How come?

Clarifying questions drill deeper to understand why buyers responded the way they did to your initial question.

Keep in mind that once you uncover all the information you need with clarifying questions, move on. Too many clarifying questions can get annoying and feel repetitive to buyers. We are not interrogating buyers; we are engaging them in a pleasant conversation.

You Know What Happens When You Assume . . .

Many times experienced sales professionals tell us it isn't a good idea to ask all those questions because their buyer will think they're inexperienced. These sales professionals assume they know what is best for their buyer even before the buyer knows. Research shows that many buyers are put off by sales professionals who assume anything about them. Most people enjoy talking about themselves; this is true with successful people and even truer with very successful people. So we must avoid assuming anything about the buyer. Rather, we must ask questions and allow the buyer to reveal the real answer. The rapport between buyer and sales professional is weakened when we assume we know what the buyer will say, even when our assumptions are 100% accurate!

Discovering Where the Emotional Criterion Is Hiding

Recall from Chapter 14 that the emotional criterion refers to "why" we want to purchase a product or service. The emotional criterion is often the primary motivator because most of us buy to satisfy our emotions and then rationalize our purchase through logic. Most buyers have never even heard the term "emotional criterion," let alone talked about it. That's why we've got to probe a little to get at it. An important key to unlocking the emotional criterion is the follow-up questions we use to dig deeper into what buyers are telling us. Our initial flow of questions certainly gets the ball rolling and we need to listen very carefully because each answer can give us a clue to a good clarifying question that will provide us with a thorough understanding of their situation.

What If You Sell Boring Products?

You may think that finding the emotional criterion is fine if you sell exciting products like cars, houses, financial services, yachts, or travel. But what if you sell a very ordinary, uninspiring product? For instance, what if you sell lumber, or sheet metal, or construction materials? Can we get to the emotional criterion with products like these? The answer is absolutely! We witnessed a top sales professional do a terrific job of discovery and ask great clarifying questions until he was absolutely sure he had learned his buyer's emotional criterion. And he was selling peptides to the biotech industry. Every decision we make has some type of emotional payout.

Humans are emotionally motivated beings. We tend to justify with logic what we want emotionally. It is true that many people are not completely aware of their emotional needs and others are simply not very comfortable discussing them. (Personally, I am not a touchy, feely guy who likes to discuss my emotions. My brother Paul, on the other hand, loves to touch souls.) Nevertheless, everyone has emotional needs. They're in there. It just may take some good clarifying questions to bring them to the surface.

☛ READY, AIM, FIRE!

Build Your Own Questioning Flow

Go ahead and take a few minutes to develop your own questioning flow. Think of an upcoming meeting and prepare a questioning flow you'll use to get the information you need so you can later present the buyer with a tailored solution. You can write your responses on another sheet of paper or print out the template at www.silverbulletselling.com. Remember to include current situation questions, desired situation questions, and expectation questions.

Practice Delivering Your Own Questioning Flow

The more you practice your questioning flow the more effectively you'll be able to use it. Go ahead and create your own mind map of your questioning flow on a separate sheet of paper. Use this map to help you remember the order of your questioning flow.

No doubt this is going to feel and sound awkward at first, but if you keep at it soon it will start to feel more natural.

1. Stand with your customized questioning flow in hand.
2. Read your questioning flow aloud twice verbatim, including the areas of questioning. It might sound like this:
   - Current Situation: General Business: "Jim, how long have you been in business?" (Saying the questioning area sounds funny, but saying it out loud will help you memorize the areas of questioning.)

3. Read your questioning flow four to six times slowly until you begin to memorize the questioning areas and the questions that go with them.

4. In the mirror, look yourself in the eye while delivering your questioning flow.

5. Practice saying your questioning flow until you have the questioning areas and many of the questions memorized.

6. Take a 30-minute break.

7. Repeat steps 3 and 4 until your delivery is smooth and sounds uncanned.

8. Using a tape recorder, record your delivery to hear what you sound like. Assess what you hear and adjust your delivery until you are very satisfied. Make sure your tone of voice is enthusiastic, not interrogative.

After you have conducted discovery and uncovered a lot of information you can use to create a tailored solution, you want to do something that will create some positive buying momentum. And I have just the right thing. It's called the discovery summary and you'll learn all about it in the next chapter.

CHAPTER SIXTEEN

The Discovery Summary
So Important, It Gets Its Own Chapter

O ur research shows that many sales are actually made right here in the discovery summary. When the summary is done well, it accomplishes all these things:

- Buyers feel good because they know you were really paying attention and listening to what they told you.
- You build momentum by distilling what has just taken upward of 60 minutes into a powerful 2-minute highlight reel.
- You ensure that your understanding of your buyer's situation is crystal clear and on target. If, for some reason, you did not summarize the situation accurately, your buyer will correct you.
- You get to show your buyer that you are a highly competent professional who understands and cares about his situation.
- You lower your buyer's resistance and raise his receptivity to your tailored solution.
- Sometimes the discovery summary even uncovers a nugget that defines the buying gap.

> ## $500 Sales Tip!
>
> It is critical for the discovery summary to be pinpoint accurate. Taking good notes will prepare you to deliver a discovery summary with a powerful punch.
>
> —G.A. Bartick

The discovery summary is all that; it really is. Not bad for a simple summary that takes less than 120 seconds to deliver, eh? But like everything else with Bullet Selling, it's all in the execution.

Discovery Summary: Taking Discovery to the Next Level

So there I was sitting at the world headquarters of Oakley Sunglasses in Foothill Ranch, California. It's quite a complex. It sits on top of a hill and looks like a castle complete with turrets and the Jolly Roger flag flying high above. My favorite part is the NBA regulation basketball court right in the center of the complex.

I was there on a sales call to meet with Dale, the Vice President of Sales. I followed my Bullet Selling process. I did my pre-call planning. I showed up right on time for the appointment and started the meeting with some preliminary pleasantries. Then I moved into the business conversation and built rapport using my agenda statement and my 90-second credibility statement. I followed with my discovery questions and we discussed his team's current situation, desired situation, and expectations of a consulting partner.

During the conversation I took detailed notes using a mind map and I referred to them as I launched into my discovery summary. When I was done recapping Dale's situation and expectations, I asked him a simple question. "Dale, is there anything I might have missed?" And what came next was the gold nugget I needed to make the sale. Dale said, "G.A., to tell you the truth, I was brought in here just over a year ago to increase sales and, as of now, sales have been flat. If I do not increase sales I am a bit concerned for my job." BINGO! Buying gap identified! What was my solution going to help Dale do? It was going to show him how he was going to keep his job. I went back to my office and wrote up a proposal that I presented to Dale the following week. During the solution presentation meeting we discussed how the program would increase sales and ultimately save his job. When Dale called me the next week and told me he was going to go with OutSell, I asked him why he had chosen us. He said, "It was obvious you understood my situation better than anyone else."

What did I do differently than my competition to give Dale this impression? I've got to believe it was the discovery summary.

Delivering the Discovery Summary

Delivering the summary is a blast when you nail it and move the sale forward. Why then do so few sales professionals give a quick recap before moving to the next step of the sales process? That's a good question. Maybe it's because most people don't know about it, or maybe it's because of the risk involved in giving a discovery summary. Delivering a summary puts pressure on us to really listen, take good notes, and then prove we understand. We have to perform and a lot of people just don't want to work that hard. By delivering an effective discovery summary we can really set ourselves apart from the competition.

To help with the delivery of the discovery summary, think of it as six separate steps:

1. Transition into the summary
2. Review the current situation
3. Review the desired situation
4. Review the expectations
5. Ask confirming questions
6. Transition to the Tailored Solution step

$500 Sales Tip!

When I take notes on my mind map, I put a star
next to the key points I want to include in my
discovery summary. That way all I need to do is
quickly glance down at my mind map to move
through my summary.

—G.A. Bartick

Steps #1 and #2: Transition into the Summary and Review the Current Situation

We use a transition phrase that first thanks our buyer for sharing all of
that valuable information with us. Then the transition moves us out of the
question-asking phase of the Discovery step into the discovery summary.
After the transition phrase, we recap the buyer's current situation.

> **Transition Phrase**
>
> *Bill, thanks for sharing all that valuable information with me. I would like to quickly
> review what we talked about just to make sure I really understand your situation . . .*
> • Review current situation information.

Step #3: Review the Desired Situation

We use another transition phrase to move into the recap of the desired
situation. You will also insert your title (e.g., financial advisor, broker, sales
professional, relationship manager, sales rep) in the transition phrase.

> **Transition Phrase**
>
> *You would like to work with a (insert your title) to help you achieve the following . . .*
> • Review desired situation information.

Step #4: Review Expectations

We use yet another transition phrase to move into the recap of your buyer's expectations.

> **Transition Phrase**
>
> *What you expect of your* (insert your title or product) *is* ...
> • Review expectations.

Step #5: Ask Confirming Questions

We ask two key questions. The first is to make sure our discovery summary is accurate. The second is a trial close that asks buyers if they would consider working with us if we could help them realize their desired situation. This is the very first true "buying" question we ask. If buyers say yes here, that is a fantastic buying signal. If a buyer hesitates, we have the opportunity to ask why. We'll cover how we address concerns in Chapter 21.

> **2 Key Questions**
>
> *Can you think of anything important I might have missed?*
>
> *So if I could put together a program that will enable you to* (insert desired situation), *would you be willing to look at a proposal and consider working with me and* (insert company)?

Step #6: Transition to the Tailored Solution Step

We use our final transition to exit the Discovery step and move into the Tailored Solution step.

> **Transition Phrase**
>
> *Great, what I suggest we do at this point is…*

If the next step is to prepare a proposal for your buyer, suggest scheduling a date to present the proposal. If this is the case, I always ask if I can call or e-mail if I need more information to complete the proposal.

If you have a solution at the ready, just transition by saying that you're ready to talk about what you can do for them.

Example Discovery Summary

Here is an example of a summary, from start to finish, that I might deliver in my business when I am working with a sales executive.

> **Steps #1 & #2: Transition into Summary & Review Current Situation**
>
> *Bill, thank you for sharing all of your valuable insights with me. I would like to do a quick recap of what we learned to make sure I really understand your situation. You have a nationwide sales force of about 250 people organized into five different regions with five regional VPs of Sales heading each region. Over the last three years sales have increased an average of about 4% per year, which is well below your target. You feel your products and services are strong and you have tremendous customer loyalty as evidenced by the research study you showed me. Your turnover with your sales force is relatively low and you feel there are some bottom performers who should probably have been managed out by now that are hurting results. For whatever reason, several of your regional VPs are reluctant to manage their sales teams for higher performance and that frustrates you.*
>
> **Step #3: Review Desired Situation**
>
> *You would like to work with a consulting organization to help you achieve your growth target of 11% a year for the next two years. This is one of your primary goals. In addition, if results improve, you're in a much better position to offer incentives. You want a performance-based sales management system built to support a comprehensive sales training program and you want it completely customized to your company, your products and services, and your sales cycle. And if this all can be achieved, it would position you as a strong candidate for the open Executive Vice President position.*

Step #4: Expectations

What you expect from your training and consulting partner is a company with the experience and expertise in your niche market, and you want to make sure the people who deliver the project to your team have earned the right to tell some very experienced and tenured sales professionals and managers what to do. You also want to make sure the company you work with is able to do regional follow-up out in the field. Then you want the company to report back to you about how well the program is being executed and make recommendations to improve performance even more.

Step #5: Ask Confirming Questions

Does that accurately sum up your situation? Can you think of anything important I might have missed? (Wait for buyer to response)

If I could put together a program that will enable your team to execute more effectively in the field so you can reach your sales growth goal of 11% per year, would you be willing to look at a proposal and consider working with me and OutSell?

Step #6: Transition to Tailored Solution

Great, what I suggest we do at this point is let me get to work on a customized proposal. I can have that ready and present it to you on Friday. Does that work for you?

Ideally, the buyer is bobbing his head up and down thinking "Wow, this guy gets it! He really understands us. In fact, I think he understands our situation better than some of our regional VPs do." And when that happens the buyer is emotionally invested and hopes that you can come up with a good solution. If you do, you've got a very good shot at getting the deal because you have communicated and articulated his situation more effectively than anyone else. When you really get good at delivering discovery summaries, buyers will say that you summarize their situations better than they can. And that is how you forge an emotional connection and build momentum and excitement!

A Few Choice Words about Sales Cycles

The steps of the sales process are the same whether you sell a product or service that can be sold in one visit or you need ten visits to close the deal. When you are in a short sales cycle, at the end of the discovery summary simply bridge into your solution with a phrase like:

- *Great, what I suggest we do at this point is talk a little about what we can do to help you achieve the goals you shared with me.*

This phrase helps transition you to the next step of the sales process: the Tailored Solution.

What about Long Sales Cycles?

In long-cycle selling you will probably need to do some work on a proposal, a bid, or some type of offer document. When this is the case, it is critical that you schedule the solution presentation meeting right there. This is one of the most important rules to remember in long-cycle selling. *Schedule your next appointment during your discovery meeting.* Doing so can significantly reduce the amount of time it will take you to close a deal because you will eliminate all that dead time between meetings. Our research shows that the time required to close a sale dramatically decreases when a date is set to deliver the tailored solution right there at the end of the discovery meeting.

$500 Sales Tip!

Warm prospects cool off quickly. A quickly scheduled follow-up meeting or solution presentation is a great way to keep your prospect's attention focused on you.

—G.A. Bartick

All too often sales professionals in long-cycle sales leave the meeting saying something like, "Thank you for your help today. I'd like to work on some ideas and then call you when we've got a proposal. How does that sound?" Of course the buyer says that's great, but nothing is on the calendar. Then all too often, either: (1) the development of the proposal lags because there is no hard deadline established, or (2) a couple of rounds of phone tag transpire as you try to set up a meeting. Either way, you lose. Don't let it happen to you. Close every meeting by closing for the next meeting. By doing this you will also find out whether the sale is moving forward. If the buyer is reluctant to schedule a follow-up meeting, he's telling you the sale is in trouble. Closing for the next appointment is critical.

Discovery Tips

1. Limit your own talking; you can't talk and listen at the same time. Listen, listen, and then listen some more!

2. Actively listen to your buyer by occasionally nodding your head and giving audio cues.

3. Remember what matters most to your buyer is the fulfillment of his desired situation. You need to capture the essence of what that is.

4. Start discovery with less threatening questions about the buyer's current situation. Move to the desired situation once you have earned the right to ask these more difficult questions.

5. Take accurate notes using the mind-mapping technique so that you are able to do an accurate discovery summary.

6. Discovery is an ongoing process, not an event. Every time you talk with your buyer, you should be gathering pertinent information.

7. Discovery could happen anytime. It could happen in a 5-minute conversation or during a 45-minute strategic appointment.

8. Think like your buyer. He has problems, needs, and wants that are important. You'll understand them better if you try to see

his points of view. Listen to understand instead of listening to respond. (Try this at home too!)

9. Resist the impulse to give your solutions until you fully understand your buyer's situation.

10. Prepare questions in advance and write them on a mind map. In fact, put this on your pre-call planning checklist. Questions prepared in advance free your mind for listening. Don't fall into the trap of developing the next question while your buyer is speaking.

Tailored Solution

1. Pre-Call Planning
2. Building Rapport
3. Discovery
4. **Tailored Solution**
5. Addressing Concerns
6. Closing the Sale

CHAPTER SEVENTEEN

Tailored Solution Overview

Building a tailored solution around what you learned in discovery is key. How you communicate your tailored solution is double key.

—G.A. Bartick

The Tailored Solution Defined

Q: What does it mean to tailor a solution?

A: The tailored solution is taking what you learned about your buyers in discovery and building a solution that bridges their current situation with their desired situation. The tailored solution consists of two parts. One part is an entirely customized solution to buyers' wants, interests, and needs. The second part is an intelligent strategy to communicate the solution presentation so that buyers understand exactly how it will move them from their current situation to their desired situation.

Q: Why is tailoring a solution so important?

A: The tailored solution gives you the opportunity to close more sales because it allows you to create a unique and different buying experience for each buyer by customizing the solution to meet the exact individual needs of each one.

After you complete the Discovery step, you are ready to move to your solution presentation. This is where you take everything you have learned about your buyer and transform his goals, needs, issues, problems, and concerns into a compelling reason to buy from you. In the Tailored Solution step, you have to know what to say whether it is in the form of a proposal, a bid, an estimate, or simply an on-the-spot solution. But it's not enough to know what to say; you also need to know how to say it. You need to be able to communicate your solution so your buyer understands precisely how it satisfies his needs and helps him bridge the gap between his current and desired situations. This is where you get to show off your selling prowess.

Where We Are in the Process

The Tailored Solution step begins the second half of the Bullet Selling process. The first half of the process—Pre-Call Planning, Building Rapport, and Discovery—is entirely focused on preparing us for this exact moment, the solution presentation. Our job in the first three steps is to project a professional and competent image, build rapport, reduce resistance, increase receptivity, and learn as much as we can about the buyer's current situation, desired situation, and expectations. If we do all of these things effectively, the buyer will be ready to listen to our tailored solution.

Could You Be Better. . .

At building and communicating a tailored solution?

Could you be better at . . .

Y N Tailoring your solutions to your buyers' wants, interests, and needs?

Y N Communicating your solution so it is crystal clear how it will move buyers from their current situation to their desired situation?

Y N Communicating the business principles that drive your behavior and decisions?

Y N Differentiating yourself from your competition?

Y N Developing proposals and other solution documents that really hit the mark?

Y N Building perceived value of you, your company, and its products and services?

Y N Using evidence effectively in your solution presentation?

A Bullet from G.A.'s Chamber

One Saturday afternoon my wife Kelly and I were looking for a new car. Understand that Kelly is probably the most competent person I know, but she hates buying cars so I usually handle the deal. We were on a dealer lot on this particular Saturday and looking inside a vehicle. You know the drill. She was in the car behind the wheel and I was pushing the buttons on the dash. We were both looking forward pretending that we're tooling down the road when a sales professional interrupted and asked if we needed any help. We introduced ourselves and told him we were looking for a new car for Kelly. The sales professional shook my hand and said, "Great. As a matter of fact, the car you're looking at is the exact same car I drive myself, except mine is silver. I don't know if you know this car has: all-time four-wheel drive, a 357-horsepower engine, and towing capacity of 7,000 pounds. I tow my boat with it to the river all the time. I love mine! Would you like to take it for a test drive?"

My wife, unmoved, replied, "No thank you." We went home car-less that weekend.

The next Saturday Kelly and I were back at the same dealership shopping for cars when another sales professional came up and asked if we needed any help. We introduced ourselves and told him we were in the market for a new car for Kelly.

He introduced himself and asked, "Before I show you anything, is it okay with you if I ask a few questions?"

Being a buyer who appreciates a good sales professional, I told him to bring it on.

He asked us if there was anything that we absolutely needed in the new car. I said, "Well, yes there is. We need the car to seat seven."

Being the good sales professional he was, he asked a good clarifying question: "Why is that so important?"

I told him, "It's because we have two kids and, as you can see, one on the way. We need room for our expanding family and all the carpool shuttling Kelly does."

He then asked if there was anything else we absolutely needed.

"Well, yes there is," I responded. "We need rear air conditioning."

"Why is that so important?"

"Because we like to take trips during the summer to see my mother up in San Luis Obispo and there's nothing worse than having the kids all hot and sweaty in the back asking every five minutes, 'Are we there yet?!'"

The sales professional said, "Great. Is there anything else?"

I thought for a minute and added, "Well, yes there is. It needs to have an outside temperature thermometer."

And again the sales professional asked, "Why is that so important?"

I shrugged and said, "My wife's eight months pregnant. If she wants to know how hot it is outside, I'd just let her."

"Sounds good. Anything else?"

I couldn't think of anything else. Then the sales professional walked us over to a vehicle and said, "This car might be what you're looking for. If you notice it seats seven, which is great for Mrs. Bartick so she can carpool to swim meets and soccer games, or wherever else your children want to go with their friends. If you look over here, you can see the rear air vents. This will be fantastic for you on those hot summer trips up to Grandma's. You and your wife can enjoy the beautiful scenery and the kids won't be bugging you every five minutes because they are cool and calm in the back. And look right over here at the lower corner of the rearview mirror. There's a digital thermometer, which I know you will appreciate because you will always be able to tell how hot it is outside. In addition, it has a compass, which will be important for you, Mr. Bartick, because you will always know which direction you're headed and won't have to stop for directions. How does this all sound to you? Would you like to take it for a test drive?"

Is that car sitting in my driveway right now? You bet it is. By the way, this car also has all-time four-wheel drive, 357 horses, and can tow 7,000 pounds. It was the very same car we were looking at the week earlier. But those features didn't matter to me or my wife.

Our research shows us that most sales professionals talk about the features of their products and services because they don't take the time to learn what's important to their buyers. The second sales professional at the car dealership was able to make the sale because he built value by tailoring the benefits of the car to what we were looking for.

Why did I need a car that seats seven? To carry all my kids around. But why does Brian Quinn, who's a Senior Consultant at OutSell and recently married, need a car that seats seven? To cruise with his posse, of course. The same feature has different benefits for different people. To be effective we need to uncover what features our buyers are looking for and, more importantly, how those features are going to benefit them through good discovery questions. Then we must build those features and benefits right into our tailored solution.

The Solution Presentation: Not Your Father's Sales Presentation

Everyone understands what it means to make a sales presentation. Essentially, it is the part of the sales process where we present the capabilities of our product/service, how they will benefit our buyer, and show why he should buy from us. But even though we all agree on what a solution presentation is, there are very different ways of going about it that produce vastly different results.

Back in the day, sales presentations were built around the capabilities of a company's products and services and the sales professional's job was to sell those capabilities. Most sales presentations were full of features of the product and little, if any, tailored benefits for the buyer. Our approach is different; our solution presentation is built around the needs of the buyer. Solution presentations must sound to each buyer as if it is tailor-made for his situation. Like most things, this is easier to understand than to execute, but the Bullet Selling process will help you do both.

Buyers Buy Benefits, Not Features

Buyers buy benefits, but most sales professionals simply sell features. How come? Because that is what they have been taught. Many companies spend a great deal of time and energy teaching their sales force all the intricate features of their products.

Our research shows that buyers do not really care how a product works. Rather, they care if the product is going to solve a problem or help them get to their desired situation. For example, I don't care to know how a new software program works. But I do want to know if it is going to allow me to manipulate my e-mail and contacts so I can work more efficiently. Like most everyone else, I buy benefits, not features. Most sales professionals, however, do not take the time during discovery to truly understand their buyers, and all they have to talk about during their solution presentation is their product's features.

The Four Parts of the Solution Presentation

There are four different parts of the solution presentation:

1. Introducing the solution presentation with an agenda statement
2. Reviewing the discovery summary
3. Presenting your business philosophy
4. Presenting the details of your solution

To be effective, you have to know what to say and how to say it for each of the four parts of the presentation. In Chapters 18 through 20, I will introduce you to several tools and techniques that will help you nail each part of the solution presentation and close more sales.

CHAPTER EIGHTEEN

Your Solution Presentation Agenda Statement

Single-Call versus Multiple-Call Close

In some selling situations, the solution presentation is delivered during the initial meeting; this is the single-call close. In other situations it is more effective to schedule a follow-up meeting to present the solution; this is the multiple-call close. For multiple-call closes, sales professionals must complete a series of tasks before they are prepared to present the solution. These tasks might include:

- Conducting additional research and analysis
- Conducting additional discovery interviews
- Meeting executives of the company
- Preparing a proposal document to present during the solution presentation
- Setting up a solution presentation meeting that might include additional buyers or people from your company
- Bringing in additional people from your company to provide targeted expertise

Whether you are in a single- or multiple-call sales environment, the solution presentation utilizes exactly the same tools and techniques. In the multiple-call situation, you simply have more time to prepare. During the Tailored Solution step, we will discuss the tools and techniques that will help you to be much more effective at presenting your solution, including:

- Communicating the solution agenda statement
- Reviewing the discovery summary
- Communicating your business philosophy with the 3×3 presentation technique
- Presenting the details of your solution
- Building value with links, features, bridges, and benefits
- Utilizing evidence
- Using trial closes

Begin the Solution Presentation with an Agenda Statement

The solution presentation needs to begin with a brief outline of what you are going to cover during the meeting. This is even true when you are presenting the solution during the initial sales call. The Bullet Selling solution presentation agenda statement follows the exact same POINT setup as the agenda statement we learned in Chapter 10.

1. **P**urpose: Discuss the purpose of the meeting
2. **O**utline: Briefly outline what you are going to cover in your presentation
3. **IN**put: Ask your buyer if there are any other areas he would like you to cover
4. **T**ransition: Transition to the first agenda item (usually a quick recap of the previous meeting)

Here's an example of how that might work in the medical supplies industry (multiple-call close) and the beauty supply industry (single-call close).

Medical Supplies Industry (Multiple-Call Close)

Purpose:

> Julie, thanks for having me back to the office. The purpose of getting together this morning is to present and discuss our solution for the medical supply needs of the orthopedic unit at Boston General.

Outline:

> I'd like to start off by:
>
> - Reviewing what we discussed during our last meeting and what has happened since.
> - Then I'd like to share my overall business philosophy with you.
> - And then move into talking about some specific ideas I have about how best to take care of your medical supply needs.
> - And finally I'd like to respond to any questions you might have.

Input:

> Is there anything else you'd like to cover?
> (Write down whatever your buyer wants to cover until he has no more agenda items.)

Transition:

> Excellent, then let's begin by quickly reviewing what we discussed in our last meeting.

Beauty Supply Industry (Single-Call Close)

Purpose:
> *Jessica, thanks for sharing all that information with me. Based on what you told me I believe Bella can help build your salon business.*

Outline:
> • *I'd like to begin by telling you about my overall business philosophy.*
>
> • *Then I'll move into some product and training recommendations I have for you based on what you told me.*
>
> • *And finally I'd like to respond to any questions you might have.*

Input:
> *Is there anything else you'd like to discuss?*
> (Write down whatever your buyer wants to cover until he has no more agenda items.)

Transition:
> *Then let's start by talking about my business philosophy and how that philosophy helps create success for our clients.*

Click Here!

To see more examples of agenda statements from different industries, visit our web site at silverbulletselling.com.

The What and the Why

Even though these two agenda statements are similar, you might have noticed the extra step in the outline of the long-cycle example. When you are presenting your solution on a different day than you conducted your discovery, it is critical to start the meeting with the discovery summary you delivered at the end of the discovery meeting. You must do this because it:

- Refocuses your buyer on his current and desired situation
- Reminds him of how professional, competent, and prepared you are
- Ensures that your buyer is on the same page as you are
- Generates positive momentum before you present your solution
- Allows other meeting participants who have not been part of the process to understand what has led up to the solution presentation

The Discovery Summary All Over Again

The first agenda item in multiple-call situations is going to be a quick review of what you discussed during your last meeting. Think of this as an opportunity for an encore performance for your discovery summary, but this time you end the discovery summary with two simple questions.

1. *Does that accurately sum up what we discussed last time?*
2. *Has anything changed?*

The second question is key. If something fundamental has changed since your last meeting, you'd better find out about it right now. It may affect how you present your solution. In fact, I've pulled proposals off the table to rework them based on the new information I learned from this question.

Obviously, you don't need to do this if you're making the solution presentation immediately after discovery because your buyer will have just heard your summary.

After this piece of the solution presentation, you are ready to move on to your business philosophy.

CHAPTER NINETEEN

Your Business Philosophy

Building Your Business Philosophy

As you did with your discovery flow, you will be more effective at presenting your solution if you begin with general points that are easy for your buyer to agree with. This is why we strongly suggest you begin your solution presentation with your business philosophy, which is built around three key points. Your business philosophy differentiates you from your competition because it tells your buyer the principles that guide the way you do business.

Impact of Your Business Philosophy

Delivering a powerful and interesting business philosophy is an important component of the Bullet Selling process. If you do it effectively, your buyer will come to some favorable conclusions very early into your solution presentation. For example, your buyer may think:

- This person believes in the same things I do.
- I like the way this person thinks.
- I appreciate that this person is passionate and knowledgeable about his business values.
- I like the fact that this person has a set of principles he uses to guide his behavior and decisions.

155

- No other salesperson has ever explained his business philosophy to me before.

When your buyer begins thinking like this, he will be more receptive to everything you say.

The 3×3 Presentation Technique

We have found through our research that sales professionals who use the 3×3 technique communicate more clearly and convincingly. The technique gets its name because we package our message into three key points and then we state each point three times. We use the 3×3 presentation technique to present our business philosophy. The 3×3 technique consists of four steps:

Step 1. Introduce and preview your key points (Tell 'em what you're going to tell 'em.)

First you have to introduce your business philosophy. Then you must name each of the three points. Do not go into any detail about each point, however. You will do that in the next step.

Step 2. Explain your key points (Tell 'em.)

In this step, you provide detail about each key point and how it benefits your buyer.

Step 3. Review your key points (Tell 'em what you told 'em.)

Now restate the three key points of your business philosophy.

Step 4. Gain buyer feedback

In this step, you discover the buyer's reaction to your business principles by asking a simple but powerful question: *"Is that the type of relationship you would like to have with your financial advisor/insurance agent/etc. (fill in appropriate title)?"*

Business Philosophy Example

Here is what a business philosophy sounds like. (Note: In the example, the financial advisor uses the term "investing philosophy" instead of "business philosophy.")

Financial Services Business Philosophy

Step 1: Introduce & Preview Your Key Points
  (Tell 'em what you're going to tell 'em)

Brad, I'd like to begin by sharing my investing philosophy. This philosophy is the compass I use with every one of my clients. The three fundamentals of my investing philosophy are:
  • *Earning the right to become my client's trusted advisor*
  • *Thoroughly understanding my client's situation and goals*
  • *Educating my clients*

Step 2: Explain Your Key Points
  (Tell 'em)

Let me explain in more detail.

  1. *The first fundamental I believe in is developing long-term relationships with my clients and earning the opportunity to become their trusted advisor. This is important because I want to partner with my clients to make decisions that will benefit them and help them realize their long-term financial goals.*

  2. *The second fundamental I believe in is the need to thoroughly understand the intricacies of my clients' situation. I believe in this fundamental because meeting with my clients regularly allows me to offer them the best advice, products and services customized to my clients' needs.*

  3. *Understanding my clients' situation leads me to my third and final principle: educating my clients about all the products and services our firm offers. The Long Beach office is perfectly positioned because we can offer "big firm" products with "small firm" personalized service. This fundamental works for my clients because it's my job to make sure they thoroughly understand the suite of products and services we offer and make sure they utilize those that best serve their interests.*

Step 3: Review Your Key Points
  (Tell 'em what you told 'em)

So to quickly review, the fundamentals I apply to each client I work with are:
  • *Developing long-term relationships that evolve into me being a trusted advisor.*
  • *Understanding my clients' current and desired financial situation intimately in order to give them the best advice.*
  • *And educating my clients on our complete suite of products and services.*

Step 4: Gain Buyer Feedback

Is that the type of relationship you would like to have with your financial advisor?

Click Here!

To see more examples of business philosophies from different industries, go to www.silverbulletselling.com.

The What and the Why

Did you know...

In 1956 George Miller proved that the average person can remember five to nine items at a time.

We use the 3×3 presentation technique whenever we want to deliver a lot of information in a short period of time. The technique organizes information in a format that is easy for your buyers to remember because it reinforces the content three times. During the 3×3, you: (1) tell them what you're going to tell them, (2) tell them, and (3) tell them what you told them. This repetition commits the content to memory.

☞ READY, AIM, FIRE!

Build Your Own Business Philosophy

Business philosophies need to be passionate explanations customized to the set of business principles you believe in and live by. They should be different from industry to industry and company to company. They might even be different for sales professionals in the same company selling the same product. Spend a few minutes now developing your own business philosophy. Think of an upcoming business meeting where you will want to deliver your business philosophy.

Building Your Business Philosophy

To build your own business philosophy, first brainstorm the building blocks of this critical piece of your solution presentation.

In this brainstorming exercise write down anything that comes to mind. Do not worry about finely crafting the verbiage at this point. Quantity is more important than quality. Anything goes and, if possible, capture your thoughts in simple bullet points. This might be a good time to practice your mind mapping.

It's important for you to answer the following eight questions in writing because your answers will begin to form the foundation of your business philosophy. You can write your responses on a separate sheet of paper or use the template at www.silverbulletselling.com.

1. What do buyers tell you they like about your company?
2. What do buyers tell you they like about doing business with you?
3. What do buyers say when they compliment you?
4. What do buyers say sets you apart from the competition?
5. What values does your senior management team exhibit, talk about, and try to reinforce in your organization?
6. What values or beliefs do your company's vision and mission statement express?
7. What business principles have you read or come across over the years that you have embraced and try to incorporate into the way you do business?
8. What are the most significant benefits buyers receive when they choose to do business with you?

Organize and Develop Your Thoughts

All of this brainstorming should stir your thinking about your broad business philosophy. The next step is to take all of this information and organize it effectively. In other words, put like ideas together so that you have a list of core business philosophy topics. You may prefer to review all that you have written down and summarize like ideas onto a new sheet of paper. The key here is to create a list of three to seven "big topic areas."

Next, rank each of the big topic areas. This means that you put a "1" next to the most important topic, a "2" next to the second most important topic, and so on. Right now you're probably thinking that they are all important, and they probably are. However, it is critical to determine, from your own viewpoint, the rank order of each of your important beliefs/fundamental values. You're done with this step when each big topic area has a number by it.

Then star (*) the three principles you rank as most important. These are the three fundamentals your business philosophy is built on. Then take each fundamental and develop it with a paragraph that describes how it benefits your buyers.

☛ READY, AIM, FIRE!

Practice Delivering Your Own Business Philosophy

Top sales professionals practice their craft because they know practice is the only way to improve their game. Take a few minutes right now to practice your business philosophy.

1. Stand up with your customized business philosophy in hand.
2. Read your business philosophy aloud twice verbatim, including the steps of the process.
3. Read your business philosophy four to six times aloud slowly, until you begin to memorize the process (not the words, but the steps).
4. Practice repeating your business philosophy until you have the process memorized and can communicate it without your notes.
5. Take a break.
6. Repeat steps 3 and 4 until your delivery is smooth and uncanned.
7. Using a tape recorder, record your delivery to hear what you sound like. Assess what you hear and adjust your delivery until you are very satisfied. Make sure your tone of voice is enthusiastic, not monotone.

Building Your Reserve Power

Now that you've developed the most important three principles, develop two more. Why? Because you'll need to customize which fundamentals you'll include in your business philosophy based on a buyer's current situation and desired situation. Developing five principles will build your Reserve Power.

On a separate sheet of paper (or on the template you can download from www.silverbulletselling.com), go ahead and write down the two additional fundamentals and develop each of them with a paragraph that describes how they benefit your buyers.

Too Much Information

If you want to develop an effective business philosophy, you must extract the most important three ideas. You may have five absolutely fabulous big-topic areas, but it would take you five minutes to explain each of those key points clearly. By the time you do this, your buyer's eyes would be glazed over from too much information. Or you might try to squeeze all five points into a 90-second presentation, and that isn't very effective. Great communicators organize their message in a way that is easy to understand and assimilate. They do this by distilling the message down into several key points and then illustrating each point effectively.

Test Buyer's Reaction to Your Business Philosophy

After you present your business philosophy, it is important to test your buyer's reaction to what he has just heard. Here are a few example questions you can try:

- *Does this sound like the type of company you like to do business with?*
- *Is that the type of relationship you would like to have with your (insert your title)?*
- *Is this type of business philosophy compatible with what you are looking for from the suppliers you work with?*

If your buyer responds positively, your solution presentation is off to a great start. The whole reason you start your solution presentation with your business philosophy is to build momentum by gaining your buyer's agreement that this is the right way to do business. Too often sales professionals put a proposal in front of a buyer and the conversation quickly moves toward the page with the financial figures on it. More often than not, you'll have better luck if you begin with general information that your buyer will immediately agree with.

What If Your Buyer Disagrees with Your Business Philosophy?

Occasionally a buyer might not respond positively to your business philosophy. However, I've got to tell you that I've never seen a buyer say, "No, I don't want to work with a company that exhibits those well-thought-out, customized-to-my-needs fundamental values." If this ever happens, all you need to do is ask a simple question like:

- *Could you please describe to me the type of company you do like to do business with?*
- *What is missing in my business philosophy?*

Listen carefully to the answer. If it's clear that you do not share a common business philosophy, seriously consider shaking hands and walking away. In other cases, your buyer's answers will guide you to some very doable compromises resulting in a shared philosophy and a successful sale.

How Do You Compete? Figuring Out Your Competitive Advantage

Nearly every company competes for business based primarily on price, quality, or service. It is the exceptional (and very rare) company that can be the market leader in all three areas.

Companies that compete on price typically emphasize the cost savings more than other benefits. It doesn't mean they ignore service and quality altogether, but that they tend to talk more about their pricing advantages. Examples of well-known price competitors include Southwest Airlines, Wal-Mart, Jack in the Box, Dollar Rent-A-Car, Motel 6, and Best Buy. I'm sure all of these companies work hard at providing good service, and some of them—Southwest Airlines, for example—have even developed a reputation for certain service advantages, but the key to their success is driving business through highly competitive pricing. Typically, their strategy is to operate more efficiently than the competition and pass those savings on to buyers.

Many companies compete on quality rather than competitive pricing. Mercedes-Benz, Tiffany, Gucci, BMW, Sony, Nikon, Bang & Olufsen, and Allen-Edmonds are some examples. These companies communicate to consumers that their products cost more because they're worth it; buyers expect to pay a little more (and sometimes a lot more) for the products they perceive to be of the highest quality.

Companies that compete on service include Nordstrom, Virgin Atlantic, American Express, Starbucks, and Four Seasons Hotels, to name a few. These companies communicate that they are dedicated to customer service and the buyer experience.

One of the findings from our research is that some top performers communicate their competitive advantage as one of their three points in their business philosophy. They believe it's important to differentiate themselves as a price leader, quality leader, or service leader.

After presenting your business philosophy, it's time to move on to the details of your solution. In the next chapter I'll explain how to build the perceived value of your products and services and deliver proposals that your buyers will want to accept.

CHAPTER TWENTY

Presenting the Details of Your Solution

Presenting the Details of the Deal

Once you've kicked off the solution presentation with your agenda statement and followed it with your discovery summary and business philosophy, it's time to dive into the fourth part of the solution presentation: communicating your specific recommendations. In many industries, you will present a written document such as a proposal, a bid, or an estimate.

Presenting the details of your recommendation is the meat of your solution presentation. Your buyer wants to know what it is and what it costs. Most of all, he wants to know if it is a good value. The key here, then, is how you explain the value.

It's All about WIIFM

In general, value perception increases when your buyer discovers the benefits he will receive. This is what I call "WIIFM" (what's in it for me)! Many research studies (including ours) show that the most effective sales professionals communicate in terms of the *benefits* of their products/services *to their buyers*. Conversely, less effective sales professionals communicate in terms of the *features* of their products/services. My car-buying experience from Chapter 17 illustrates this little nugget of wisdom.

Features, Bridges, and Benefits

Virtually every sales training program I've seen emphasizes the need to know features and benefits. Still, few sales professionals know how to use them effectively. The key is to combine a feature with a benefit and join them together with a bridge. Once you know your features, bridges, and benefits (FBBs), you can use that knowledge in a variety of ways to build value.

Features and Benefits

Features and benefits are the raw materials we use to construct value propositions. A feature is a fact, not a claim or opinion, about your product or service. A feature is most effective when it is explained accurately. When you exaggerate, you erode your credibility and lower perceived value. Here are some examples of features from a variety of industries:

- This new AXR investment account has a sweep function.
- The storage capacity of the hard drive on this computer is 30 gigabytes.
- Our company was founded in 1968.
- We currently have over 27,000 active buyers.
- We've won the J.D. Power award for best customer service the past four years running.

The Bridge

The bridge is a short phrase that connects the feature to the benefit and contains the word "you" or "your." Consider these examples:

- This will allow you to. . . .
- This gives you the ability to. . . .

- With this, your team will be able to. . . .
- This is great for you because. . . .

I could list dozens of different bridge alternatives. When you are presenting the WIIFMs, it is important to use a variety of bridges so they do not sound scripted or canned. Here's how to connect the feature to the bridge:

- This new AXR investment account has a sweep function that will help you because . . . (add benefit)
- The storage capacity of the hard drive on this computer is 30 gigabytes. This will be great for you because . . . (add benefit)
- Our company was founded in 1968 and this gives you . . . (add benefit)
- We currently have over 27,000 active buyers and this will benefit you because . . . (add benefit)

The What and the Why

Bridges help us connect the feature to the benefit in a buyer-oriented way. Using bridges with the word "you" or "your" helps to communicate how the feature will benefit each specific buyer. I cannot overemphasize the importance of this point. Watch your buyer's ears perk up when you use an effective bridge containing the word "you."

The Benefit

Benefits are how buyers experience the feature. The key to communicating benefits effectively is to phrase them in a way that is meaningful to your buyer. Look at the following FBB sentences and notice how the benefits are focused on the buyer.

FBB Statements		
Feature	*Bridge*	*Benefit*
This new AXR investment account has a sweep function	And that will help you because	Every day your money will still be receiving our high interest rates, increasing your overall return so you'll have the money at the ready when your freshman son is entering college.
The storage capacity of the hard drive on this computer is 30 gigabytes.	This will be great for you because	You can store your documents, your music, and the digital photos of your daughter's wedding right on your computer.
Our company was founded in 1968	And this gives you	The peace of mind of knowing that we've weathered tough economic times before.
We currently have over 27,000 active customers	And this will benefit you because	It allows us to reduce our operating expenses and pass those savings right back to you in the form of lower prices, which you can put right in your son's college fund.

Many sales professionals assume it is not necessary to explain benefits because they are "obvious" to the buyer. This just isn't the case. Any feature you bring up can be interpreted in a variety of ways depending on your buyer's needs and experiences. By providing an FBB statement, you are helping your buyer understand how that feature benefits him.

A very common mistake during the solution presentation is to talk too much about features and not enough about benefits. Beware of this. Buyers want to know more than just what your product or service can do; they want to know specifically what it can do for *them*.

Just Saving Time Is Not a Benefit

Do you sell a product or have products in your line that are supposed to save people time? I've purchased my share of items designed to save time, including a microwave, a fax machine, and a BlackBerry. Even with all this time I'm saving, I still don't seem to have any extra free time. That's why I'm not very eager to buy the latest time-saving gadget.

Let's suppose I was approached by a sales professional who was trying to sell me something that is going to save my project managers' time. I would tell him no thanks. But if he customized the benefit by telling me his product is going to save my project managers' time, which will be fantastic for me because (see how I snuck in that bridge?) it will allow them to spend more time marketing OutSell to new prospects, that would be a different story. You're telling me your product is going to help my team do more marketing and close more sales? Where do I sign? That's how a good FBB works.

Linking FBBs to What You Learned in Discovery

To make your FBB statement even more effective, try linking it to what you learned about your buyer during discovery. Linking is an advanced technique that further customizes the FBB to your buyer's situation. Here are some link feature bridge benefit (LFBB) statements:

LFBB			
Link	*Feature*	*Bridge*	*Benefit*
Earlier you mentioned that you want to make sure you have no "idle money" in your investment strategy.	This new AXR investment account has a sweep function	And that will help you because	Every day your money will still be receiving our high interest rates, increasing your overall return so you'll have the money at the ready when your freshman son enters college.
You told me you want to store all of your digital pictures and MP3 music files on your hard drive.	The storage capacity of the hard drive on this computer is 30 gigabytes.	This will be great for you because	You can store your documents, your music, and the digital photos of your daughter's wedding right on your computer.
You mentioned that you value long-term relationships with your key business vendors.	Our company was founded in 1968	And this gives you	The peace of mind of knowing that we've weathered tough economic times before.
During our last meeting you told me you were very price conscious.	We currently have over 27,000 active customers	And this will benefit you because	It allows us to reduce our operating expenses and pass those savings right back to you in the form of lower prices, which you can put right in your son's college fund.

These LFBBs are customized and buyer-focused. This technique can really increase the perceived value your buyer sees in you, your company, and your products and services.

Developing Your FBB Knowledge

You may not like what I am about to say, but I'll say it anyway because our research tells me it's true. The reason so many sales professionals aren't very effective at explaining their products and services in a compelling way is that they simply don't know their products and services that well. They haven't taken the time to study the features and benefits so they are limited in what they can say about them. In fact, our research shows this is especially true with tenured employees. Knowing a lot about your company because you've been there awhile is not the same as having a strong knowledge base about the features and benefits of your company and its products/services. Solace is at hand, however. If you follow these steps, you will develop the knowledge that will allow you to talk confidently and persuasively about all of your products and services.

☛ READY, AIM, FIRE!

Build Your Own FBBs

1. Make a list of the products and services you sell and rank them in terms of popularity. Put the product or service you sell most at the top of the list and begin there.

2. Gather all information on your most popular product or service, including brochures and blurbs from your company web site. Read through the material and take notes (mind map).

3. Write a list of all the features of the most popular product or service. When the list is complete, put the facts/features in order with the most important feature at the top and rank them down to the least important one.

4. Next, complete the FBB statement by adding an effective bridge and benefit to each feature. Stretch yourself. Do not settle for what is easy unless it sounds highly effective. Get feedback from people you trust.

5. Read the FBB statement and revise the writing until it sounds exactly how you want it to.

6. Memorize the list, starting at the top. Commit the features and benefits to memory by continuing to read them out loud.

7. Follow steps 2 to 6 for each of the products/services on your list.

8. Follow steps 2 to 6, focusing on the features and benefits of your company.

If you follow these directions and get to know the features and benefits of your products/services intimately, you will find it much easier to build value. You'll be much more eager to talk about your products and services because it will be easier (and fun) for you to do so. These FBB statements will become the way you build value throughout the solution presentation, including communicating the details of the deal, answering product-/service-related questions, and handling any concerns that may come up.

— — —

There I was in the TV department at Circuit City. We needed a bigger TV for our family room and Kelly determined that we should get a 36-inch screen. So I did what many people do—I checked out consumerreports.org and tore apart the Sunday paper looking for sales at the local electronics retailers. I found a 36-inch TV on sale at Circuit City for $799, so I cut out the ad, took my son Jack (then a chatty six-year-old), and headed out. Since I've spent half my life around sales professionals, I'm quite capable of throwing out some strong sales resistance if necessary. I assumed that I would have to deal with a fairly young and inexperienced employee, so I was ready.

A moment after walking through the front door, a nicely dressed and polite gentleman approached me and Jack. "Welcome to Circuit City, how are you today?" He extended his hand to Jack and introduced himself as Leonard. In typical six-year-old fashion, Jack gave him a high-five smack that you could hear throughout the store. Leonard smiled, shook my hand, and asked, "Is there anything at all that I can help you with today?" I pulled out the advertisement, told him I was there to purchase the 36-inch TV on sale today, and asked him if it was in stock. "It certainly is. Would you like to take a quick look at it first?" he asked, turning to an area of the store filled with TVs. The store had an entire display of TVs all in a row, tuned to the same show for comparison. There were about 15 different models of the same size. "Do you like football?" Leonard asked Jack.

"Yes," he replied.

"Do you like the Chargers?" Leonard asked.

"I like them because my dad does. But my favorite team is the Aztecs." (The Aztecs is the name of the San Diego State University football team . . . my alma mater.)

"I don't think the Aztec game is on television today, but I bet we can catch the Chargers." As he said this, he reached for a row of buttons on a panel and pushed one. Instantly, all of the display models switched to a football game between the Chargers and the Kansas City Chiefs. With the ad firmly in my hand and a bucketful of sales resistance at the ready, I glanced down the row of TVs. Toward the end of the row was the sale model I was looking for. As I walked down the row, the prices climbed until I got to the Sony super deluxe model at about $2,300. "Wow," I said. "Is there really that much difference between TVs? I can't imagine what would make one TV worth $1,500 more than the one in this ad." Leonard smiled warmly and replied, "I'm glad you asked that because I am one of the world's biggest TV fanatics. I know a lot about these TVs and I'd be happy to explain them to you."

"Sure," I replied.

"Look at the line on this picture screen," Leonard said, pointing to a box on the picture of the $799 TV that framed the score of the game. "Look at it closely and see how the line flashes a bit?"

Jack squished his face right up against the glass. "Yeah, I see it."

"Come over here," Leonard suggested, walking to a TV costing about $1,300. "Look at the line on this TV." As Jack and I looked closely at the TV, we noticed that it didn't have the same flickering effect as the less expensive TV. "That flickering you see on the TV in your advertisement disappears in all the TVs above this price range because of the advanced display technology. You'll appreciate this technology because it makes watching TV easier on your eyes and more relaxing."

Nice FBB, I thought. Then I looked closely at the two screens. Sure enough, there was a noticeable difference in clarity.

"Jack, come over here," Leonard said. "Look at the faces in the crowd. "See how clear and focused the picture is?" Jack leaned into the TV and looked closely. "Now come over here and look at the same spot on this TV." He was pointing to the TV we wanted to buy. "Do you see how fuzzy the picture is here?"

"Wow," Jack said. "Hey, Dad, come over here and look at this and learn!"

As I approached the TV for the comparison test, Leonard added, "What happens is that they use less effective technology on these less expensive TVs. The parts they use simply do not focus evenly across all areas of the screen." Walking back toward the more expensive TVs he continued. "When you get to this quality"—he was pointing to a TV just three from the end—"they use a unique filter that focuses the picture perfectly across the entire screen and you get a crisp, clear picture. This will be great for you and Jack because you can watch football games together in your living room on a crystal-clear screen that makes you think you're at the stadium." Well, we didn't buy the $2,300 Sony TV, but we did decide on the $1,399 Toshiba Cinema Series model because Leonard felt it was every bit as good as the Sony and we should save the money.

Leonard was a darn fine sales professional. What he did was turn complex, highly technical features into an exciting demonstration of how far technology had come since the last time I had shopped for a TV. His extensive knowledge of the features of his products and his presentation of customized benefits allowed him to tailor everything he said to my specific situation, and he was highly successful at increasing my perceived value of a relatively high-end audio/video system. The economy would never stumble if the world were filled with more Leonards, but sadly, it isn't. And that makes for one huge opportunity for the rest of us because even hardened, sales-resistant folks like me cannot resist sales professionals who know their products, are enthusiastic about them, and are able to communicate their features and benefits in a way that is easy to understand and get excited about.

Proposal Best Practices

I can't give you too much insight into the actual content of proposals because they vary so much from industry to industry. Nevertheless, here are a few pearls of wisdom I've mined from the research.

- Offer options whenever possible

    I usually suggest that proposals provide two or three different options at different price points for buyers to choose from. Buyers appreciate the choices; it makes them feel like they are buying and not being sold. And I am always surprised at how often a buyer will choose a hybrid by putting elements of two options together. I believe the best proposal is the one the buyer helps develop.

- Make it easy to say yes

    Make one of the options a dressed-down version that the buyer can say yes to relatively easily. This is especially important in industries with repeat orders. A low-cost option makes it easier to get the buyer on board so you can begin to develop the relationship, add value, and add products and services as your relationship grows. I've heard sales professionals say, "Show them the entire bracelet and let them buy the first link now."

- Put something in front of them to say yes (or no) to quickly

    Proposals are great because they give buyers something concrete to respond to. The process of writing a proposal forces you to develop half-baked ideas into viable projects. I believe the window of opportunity only opens a crack and you have to be at the ready to take advantage of that crack before it is slammed shut. If you have an idea for buyers, get it down on paper and get it in front of them.

- Big proposals lead to big sales

    I'm not talking about more pages. I'm talking about dollars. Sales professionals often ask me how to get their buyers to buy more. The answer is simple: Ask them to buy more. Some sales professionals are hesitant to ask for a large order in fear of scaring off buyers. That is why it is so important to give buyers a few options. If you know a buyer needs more of your products or services to realize his desired situation, look him in the eye and tell him so in your proposal.

$500 Sales Tip!

You cannot make big sales without big proposals.
—G.A. Bartick

- Structure is important

    The way you structure and organize your proposal is just as important as the content. I strongly recommend a structure that includes these headings:

    — *Introduction:* The introduction includes background information about your buyer and the reason for the proposal.

    — *Current situation:* This section reviews what you learned in discovery.

    — *Desired situation:* Here you review what you learned in discovery.

    — *Recommendations:* Your recommendations bridge your buyer's current and desired situations.

    — *Company information:* This section includes pertinent information about your company's history, expertise, products, services, processes, and so on.

    — *Investment analysis:* Here you review pricing information and the financial terms of the proposal.

    — *Signing page:* Include space for your buyer to ink the deal.

- Present your proposal
  - Our research shows that presenting a proposal to your buyer, either over the phone or in person (rather than e-mailing it and waiting for a response), significantly increases your closing rate.
  - When presenting a proposal, do not review the entire document. During your pre-call planning, highlight all the important pieces of the proposal you want to cover during the presentation.
- In competitive situations, be the *first* to present your proposal

  This practice goes against conventional wisdom. However, when you have a stellar proposal and present it first, you set the bar high. All the other competing proposals will be compared to yours. In fact, twice in my career I have delivered a proposal first and my buyer decided right then and there to sign the contract without hearing a presentation from another company.

How to Use Evidence

Evidence—proof that what you are saying is indeed true—is another cool tool to use during the solution presentation. It addresses these key questions or issues in the buyer's mind:

- How do I know that what you are saying is true?
- How do I know that you aren't making this up or exaggerating?
- I want to believe you, but I need proof.
- This decision is risky and I need to know that you have my best interest at heart.
- I hate to be sold!

How much evidence do you currently use when you ask a buyer to buy from you? Do you come in empty-handed, or do you have a variety of pieces that you can use?

Do you bring testimonial letters, articles about your company, statistics, or analysis that illustrate and back up key points of your solution presentation?

Or do you just wing it?

In court, attorneys present various pieces of evidence to prove the important points of their case. Evidence increases credibility and receptivity. Lack of evidence increases doubt and resistance.

Forms of Evidence

- Testimonial letters
- Buyer success stories
- Articles from credible publications
- Expert testimony
- Exhibits
- Product demonstrations
- Video demonstrations/interviews
- Company/product awards
- Effective analogies
- Statistics/surveys/studies/reports
- Brochures
- One-page product sheets

You may even come up with other forms of evidence. This is a great topic to brainstorm at a sales meeting when the whole team is together. Look for items that support the most important points you make in the solution presentation. Often sales professionals get lazy and do not take the time to put together the evidence that would make their solution presentation more credible. Don't let this happen to you.

Organize Your Evidence

Once you get all of your evidence together, organize it into an effective presentation binder. Some sales professionals like to laminate letters and articles, and others put them into plastic protective sleeves inside a three-ring binder. No matter how you do it, keep your originals safe and make high-quality color copies for the evidence book you use on sales calls. Once you get into the habit of using evidence, you'll wear out your favorite pieces.

Only rarely do I bring my entire evidence binder into a sales call. When I'm doing my pre-call planning and ironing my briefcase, I generally take only the evidence I may need in a file folder.

Trial Close: Testing for Buyer Reaction

Throughout the solution presentation it is important to keep buyers involved to get their true responses to what they are hearing. This is important for two reasons:

1. A positive response generates positive momentum.
2. A negative response allows us to take a step back and find out what is causing the reaction (often we need to drop back into the Discovery step) before moving forward in the Tailored Solution step.

Some buyers will be very responsive during the solution presentation and you will not have to proactively test their reaction. Others are harder to read. In these cases, you can use trial close questions to test their reactions. A trial close is a short, nonthreatening question that asks buyers to react to what they have just heard. Example trial close questions include:

- *How does that sound?*
- *Does that make sense?*
- *Do you see yourself using that?*
- *Do you see how that can help your situation?*
- *How does this look to you?*
- *What do you think?*

In general, it is a good idea to test buyer reaction every few minutes. Avoid talking for more than five to six minutes without giving buyers a chance to react. People have a limited attention span and testing for a reaction allows them to take a breather and get ready for the next piece of the presentation.

Usually, a negative reaction to a trial close indicates a need for follow-up with additional questions. When a negative reaction is strong, move forward to the Addressing Concerns step (we're going to cover that in the next chapter).

Put Passion into Your Solution Presentation

Here's the trick. Plug passion into the solution presentation so it literally pours out of you and into the buyer you're speaking with. Talk with more than just your voice. Put your eyes and hands into it. Put your smile into your presentation. Communicate that you are excited about the job you can do for your buyer. Don't be afraid to exhibit your enthusiasm. I think many people act in a restrained way because they are afraid of what other people would think if they saw them excited about their work. If this is your MO, then you'll never really know what you could accomplish.

Solution Presentation Tips

1. Do not assume your buyer is familiar with your products and services. Although the benefit of a specific feature may be obvious to you, it is not necessarily obvious to your buyer.

2. Tailoring is the key to the Tailored Solution step and the major benefit of using the Bullet Selling process.

3. Be enthusiastic about your products and services. Enthusiasm is a transferable emotion, but you can't transfer it to your buyer if you don't feel it yourself during the solution presentation.

4. Watch your buyer carefully during your solution presentation. When you notice positive body language, ask how he feels about

what he's hearing. When you notice negative body language, ask if he has any questions or concerns.

5. Be concise and to the point, but don't rush through the solution. Make it enjoyable for your buyer by communicating in an engaging way.

6. Evidence is critical during the solution presentation. Bring supportive materials that prove your points. Be creative. Evidence is in the morning paper, in your mailbox, on the web . . . just pay attention.

7. You communicate about 7% of your message with your words, another 38% with your tone, and about 55% with body language.

8. Remember, people buy based on the WIIFM principle. Use LFBBs to build value in your products and services through your presentation.

9. Collect a variety of buyer success stories. Write them down and review them from time to time so they are always fresh in your mind.

10. Begin every solution presentation (and every meeting) with an agenda statement.

Addressing Concerns

1. Pre-Call Planning
2. Building Rapport
3. Discovery
4. Tailored Solution
5. **Addressing Concerns**
6. Closing the Sale

CHAPTER TWENTY-ONE

Addressing Concerns Overview

Some people say the selling starts when the concerns come. I say the selling starts at hello and, when the concerns come, that is when your skills of Bullet Selling are truly tested.

—G.A. Bartick

Addressing Concerns Defined

Q: What does it mean to address concerns?

A: A concern is anything that can cause the buyer to hesitate when considering a positive buying decision. Some of these concerns are rational, some are emotional, and others fall somewhere in between. Addressing concerns means we are going to identify and respond to each concern. It doesn't mean we're going to resolve every one. We don't have to. I'll explain why in the pages to come.

Q: Why is addressing concerns so important?

A: Addressing concerns successfully allows us to remove obstacles and move the sale forward.

Could You Be Better . . .

At addressing concerns?

Could you be better at . . .

Y   N   Addressing concerns in a nonconfrontational manner?

Y   N   Listening to understand rather than listening to respond?

Y   N   Creating a unique and different buying experience for your buyer?

Y   N   Asking clarifying questions so you can better understand your buyer's concerns?

Y   N   Understanding the concern rather than getting defensive?

Y   N   Drawing out all of your buyer's concerns before responding?

Y   N   Isolating the primary concern so you can respond to it first?

As the youngest of three boys, I became very good at addressing concerns—my well-being pretty much depended on it. I'm five years younger than Paul and so many times growing up I had to address his concern of my hanging out with his friends. Think about it. At 10 or 11 years old you don't want your kid brother tagging along with you and your friends. The addressing concerns process would have come in handy back then. But I gotta tell you, the sweetest revenge of all is being his boss. How many younger brothers get to tell their older brother how much (or little, in Paul's case) their bonus is? But I regress. Let me get back to the matter at hand, addressing concerns.

If you've been in sales for any period of time, you know from experience that concerns are a natural part of the selling process. It says so in every sales book ever written and this book is no exception. But those other books don't give you a lesson on how to execute a *nonconfrontational* process for addressing concerns that works. Most books are filled with one-line responses and comebacks that are supposed to catch unsuspecting buyers off guard. This book is different; it'll help you execute a tested process to address concerns effectively. But first, you'll have to read on as I wax poetic about the finer points of addressing concerns.

You see, addressing concerns is the game within the sales game. Concerns give you the opportunity to exercise your sales skills and benefit from the resistance-repelling rapport you've built during the first four steps of the Bullet Selling process: Pre-Call Planning, Building Rapport, Discovery, and Tailored Solution. However, if you haven't done a good job up until now, I don't believe there are any one-liners or canned responses that will magically make a buyer say, "Yes, I'll take it!"

Our research confirms that buyers usually voice at least a concern or two. In most cases buyers have concerns that need to be discussed and addressed before they will be willing to move forward. These concerns come from fear, doubt, skepticism, and emotional reactions to the selling conversation. I also think they are a way for buyers to feel they are in control of the situation and not being sold.

A Bullet from G.A.'s Chamber

When I was selling real estate, I pretty much sucked at addressing concerns because I constantly committed the three cardinal sins:

1. I listened to respond instead of listening to understand.
2. I often did not give the buyer a chance to explain his concerns in detail.
3. I immediately responded to the first concern instead of probing to reveal all of the concerns and handling the most important one first.

This last faux pas was probably the most costly and the one I committed over and over. When the Gaslamp District in downtown San Diego was still more of a red-light district, I was trying to sell quarter-million-dollar condos in a complex called Trellis 5th Avenue. The condos were nice. People loved the living space, but they questioned the neighborhood. I got tired of responding to the same concern over and over and over again.

I had been working with one couple for several months who was moving from Long Beach. They were motivated buyers who had been pre-approved for a mortgage. They told me they wanted a two bedroom/two bath, with a lot of light, in a landmark building in an up-and-coming downtown neighborhood. I thought the Trellis condos would be perfect for them. I showed them a third-floor unit and they loved it, especially the chef's kitchen. They mentioned their concern about the neighborhood, but they were interested enough to ask for a second showing during the evening.

I met them on a Thursday night and they were as excited as before. They gave me some serious buying signals when they started talking about putting a bid on the unit. However, they told me they still couldn't quite get over the neighborhood. I thought to myself, "Here we go again." I immediately countered with the fact that there was a ton of investing happening in the neighborhood and that within five years their condo would be worth a whole lot more. This didn't seem to move them. So I tried creating a sense of urgency by telling them another couple was interested in the unit and that they should put in an offer. This didn't work, either; they decided not to place an offer.

About a month later during one of our regular Monday morning sales meetings, my colleague Phyllis started talking about some new clients of hers from Long Beach who just had a bid accepted at the Trellis. I couldn't believe it. After the meeting when I had settled down a bit, I asked Phyllis how she was able to succeed where I had failed. Hadn't the couple mentioned their strong concerns over the neighborhood? Phyllis told me she first showed them a unit on the fourth floor they really liked, but that they were still really concerned with the neighborhood. Then she said something that has stuck with me. Before responding to the neighborhood concern, she asked the couple if they had any other concerns. And they did. Besides the neighborhood, they wanted a better view, even if it meant a smaller living space. In fact, they told Phyllis this was an even bigger concern than the neighborhood. So Phyllis showed them a two-bedroom/one-bath unit on the sixth floor they fell in love with. That same day they gave a bid, and the owner accepted it.

This experience taught me a lot about addressing concerns. I learned not to respond to the first concern out of my buyer's mouth. I also learned that I should ask questions to draw out other concerns and then isolate which concern is the most important of all, and start there.

Two Secrets You've Got to Know before Addressing Any Concerns

Secret #1: There Are Going to Be Concerns

Our research shows that buyers raise a concern in 84% of selling interactions. Even when buyers have every intention of buying, they're going to put up some type of resistance in the form of a concern because people don't want to be sold. It's just human nature.

━━   ━━   ━━

During my less-than-spectacular Nordstrom sales career, I remember watching a couple of women walk up to a shoe display, one of them with a taupe dress in her hand. They held up the dress next to the display trying to find the right match. They came to one pair of Joan and David's and they got excited. The chocolate-colored leather went perfectly with the taupe dress. The woman holding the dress discreetly slipped on the shoe. She gushed about how comfortable it felt. The two women became even more excited when they realized the pair was on sale. I made my move when I saw the woman with the shoe in her hand reach into her purse for her credit card. The women were already sold on the shoes and I was coming in to close the deal. I approached the women and in my friendliest, most nonaggressive voice I said, "Good afternoon, ladies. Can I help you?"

"No thank you, we're just looking."

Her response floored me. The two stood there for another few minutes and then she finally approached me and asked to purchase the shoes. I knew she had every intention of buying those shoes. And that's when the realization hit me—buyers often put up resistance in the form of a concern because they want to purchase on their own terms without feeling like they are being sold.

Secret #2: We Know Their Concerns Before They Do

This secret came out of our research and it kind of surprised us. When we dug through those 36,000 pages of notes, we found over and over again that in most selling situations the same eight concerns kept coming up. I know it's hard to fathom, but these eight concerns cover about 94% of the concerns sales professionals hear whether they're selling satellite defense equipment or satellite TV service. When I'm working with a group of sales professionals on addressing concerns, the first thing I do is ask them how many concerns their buyers have. They come back with answers like "dozens," "hundreds," and someone always shouts out "it's infinite." Then I ask them to list all of the possible concerns they hear. After about two minutes a hush comes over the room as they realize the actual number of concerns is quite small. Then we organize and categorize their list and almost every time we come up with the List of Eight:

1. Cost

    Yes, this is the granddaddy of all concerns. "Cost" can mean many things. It can mean that buyers think your product or service is too expensive, or they can't afford it, or they simply do not want to pay that much for it, or they do not see the value.

2. Terms and conditions

    This is a contractual concern with the terms and/or conditions of a sale. This could mean buyers disagree with any number of things including policies, payment schedules, fees, and so on.

3. I don't need it

    This is a utility concern. The product or service does not sufficiently satisfy the wants, interests, or needs of buyers to warrant paying the asking price. The "I don't need it" concern sometimes means "it won't work" or "it's not right."

4. I have to think about it

    This concern could literally mean that buyers have to mull the decision over. Sometimes buyers use this concern as a stalling tactic for extra time to consider other options (such as another offer from the competition) or to avoid the buying conversation and let you (the sales professional) down easy.

5. The hassle factor

    This concern may come up in the form of "I don't want to have to change vendors (companies, products)" or "I do not have the resources right now to deal with the change."

6. Experience

    The experience concern could mean several different things. Buyers could raise a concern about lack of experience or knowledge of your company. Brand awareness plays a key role here. This concern could also relate to your own experience (or lack thereof) in the company or in the industry.

7. I have to talk to my colleague/boss/spouse

    This may be a sign that you are not talking to the decision maker. More often, though, it is a simple stall tactic. As far as concerns go, this is one of my favorites. In Chapter 23 I'm going to show you how to knock this one out with one simple question.

8. I had a previous bad experience

    Buyers may be referring to an experience with your company, another company, or the product/service.

This list covers nearly all concerns which is great for you because that means your buyers' concerns are predictable. You can figure out the concerns your buyers will have even before they bring them up. This way you can be at the ready to address them. Take the time to really get good at the Bullet Selling addressing concerns process. Once you are, you can use the process effectively and close more sales for the rest of your career.

Addressing Concerns Is the Art of Selling

At this point in the sales process you've done a great job at building rapport and establishing credibility. You've asked relevant questions that have given you a clear picture of the buyer's current situation, desired situation, and expectations. The buyer knows you understand his unique situation because you delivered a spot-on discovery summary. You used what you learned to present a highly tailored business philosophy and solution. The buyer knows how your products and services will benefit him specifically because you've linked them to his desired situation with a few beautifully communicated link, feature, bridge, benefit statements.

It would be great at this point if your buyer responded by saying "Wow, that sounds great. There's no need to talk about this anymore because we've made a decision to move forward with your computer servers and, frankly, I can't see any reason why we shouldn't double the size of the order. Servers for everyone! And by the way, I've also got a few referrals for you, but let me call them first to pave the way for you." That would be wonderful, but we know this is only going to happen to those of us living in a fantasy world.

What's really going to happen is that you're going to ask for the order and the buyer is going to raise some concerns. It happens 84% of the time. We know its coming. Any decision a buyer makes involves risk, and risk makes people uncomfortable. And when people are uncomfortable, they hesitate. In addition, by saying yes to you your buyer may have to say no to someone else or, worse, tell the person who is currently providing the product or service that he no longer has their business.

But wait—there's more for the buyer to feel nervous about . . . a lot more. The buyer will have to figure out a way to pay for it and then there's the risk of buyer's remorse setting in if it turns out to be a poor decision. In some cases the buyer may have put himself at political risk in his organization by choosing you. By saying yes to you, he may literally be putting his job on the line.

So I ask you, why do people present us with concerns? Because the entire business of buying creates anxiety. And what can we do about it? Plenty. This is where the art of Bullet Selling really kicks in!

Two Situations We Don't Want to Get Into

Many sales professionals make matters worse by disagreeing with their buyer. This only increases resistance and creates conflict. Hear this: YOU CAN NEVER WIN A TUSSLE WITH A BUYER. Buyers are not going to say "uncle" just because you have some well-rehearsed, canned response to their concerns. Even when we win the logical argument, we can lose the emotional one and lose the sale. Game over. So just don't do it. The Bullet Selling process will help you avoid this pitfall.

Sometimes, after presenting our solution, we get bombarded with concerns. The truth is, if we're getting serious resistance at this point we probably did not do a very good job in the first four steps of the Bullet Selling process. If that's the case, I do not know anything that can save us. We've botched the sale and the shower of concerns is our just reward.

How the Real Pros Do It

When we were trying to figure out how top performers addressed concerns, we observed them in the field and interviewed them. We were eager to capture their intelligent responses and the one-liners they used to address concerns. Then something happened that we were not expecting. These sales professionals did not have canned responses. Instead, they asked more questions to make sure they completely understood the concern, then responded by building perceived value using information they learned in the previous four steps of the process.

Two Skills to Master

There are really only two things to master when it comes to addressing concerns:

1. Identifying the concern(s)
2. Responding effectively to the concern(s)

We'll start the next chapter by identifying some effective techniques for finding all of the concerns and worries that stall a buyer's buying decision. Then we'll learn how to prioritize them and respond effectively to each and every one if necessary.

CHAPTER TWENTY-TWO

Executing the Addressing Concerns Process

Many sales professionals approach concerns the same way they approach fishing. When the fish takes the bait, the sales professional pulls hard and reels it in, fighting the fish all the way to the boat. This is an exhausting (and exhilarating) struggle. Sometimes the fish is caught, but sometimes it gets away before we can land it and bring it onto the boat. Similarly, sometimes when buyers hit us with a first concern we strike and work hard to overcome it, thinking that if we can just "land" this concern, we can bring in the sale. Sounds good in theory, but often it doesn't work because, as I've mentioned, the initial concern isn't always the primary reason the buyer isn't biting. Instead, we need to cast a wide net so we can pull up as many concerns as possible before responding to any of them.

The Six-Step Addressing Concerns Process

Let's take a look at the six steps of the Bullet Selling addressing concerns process.

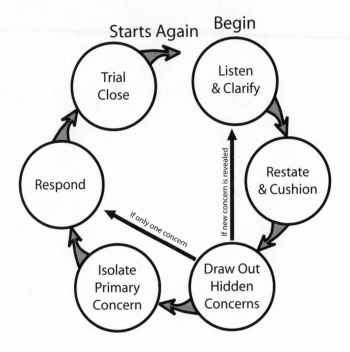

The Process Is Not Bulletproof

This process is not called the "resolving concerns process" because, quite frankly, it's impossible to resolve or fix every concern a buyer may have. You may not be able to lower the price 15% or ship the product in less than two weeks as requested. Therefore, you may lose the sale. In all of our research, in all of our data, in all of the sales calls we've been on, and working with some of the top sales professionals in the business, we have not yet found a (legal) process that works every time. Thus, our goal is not to resolve every concern; rather, we should focus on *addressing every concern* effectively. When we address concerns effectively, even if we don't resolve them, the process can move forward to a sale.

What I'm sharing with you is, by far, the most effective way to address concerns that we have come across. When executed effectively, it works very well. Can you come up with a what-if scenario where it won't work? Absolutely! Every time I teach a class there is always one participant who says, "G.A., that all sounds good, but what if the buyer says . . .?" I agree. There are going to be situations when you will execute this process flawlessly and the buyer will still not buy. That's just the way it is. Deal with it. Learn the process.

Transitioning to the Addressing Concerns Process with a Trial Close

If you recall, we concluded the Tailored Solution step with a trial close that looked something like these examples:

- *How does that sound?*
- *Does that make sense?*
- *Do you see yourself using that?*
- *Do you see how that can help your situation?*
- *How does this look to you?*
- *What do you think?*

After hearing your trial close questions, buyers are going to respond in one of four ways.

The Four Types of Buyers

We can classify buyers into four groups.

1. *Committed buyers* have no real concerns. They want your product or service and are ready to do business. It's a done deal!
2. *Unconvinced buyers* have real concerns they want you to address. They are sincerely interested in moving forward, provided you address their issues effectively. Not quite a done deal.

3. *Not-completely-honest buyers* do not express any real concerns but are not ready to commit and move forward either. Often they'll say things like:

- "I need some time to think about it."
- "I'll look into this a little closer and get back to you."
- "I need to run this by (insert anybody)."

These are difficult buyers to close because they are probably not telling you the whole truth, and it is very difficult to address concerns and close sales effectively when buyers don't open up and tell you what is really on their minds. Deal or no deal?

4. *Unattainable buyers* have made up their minds that they are not going to do business with you. Unattainable buyers may or may not raise concerns, but they make it clear they're not buying. No deal!

We know going in that we can't make every sale. It is much better to get a firm "no" from unattainable buyers early in the sales process than a hopeful "maybe." Maybes choke and clog your sales pipeline. Sales professionals who spend too much time with buyers who will never buy invite time management problems and eventual failure. The addressing concerns process allows you to smoke out these unattainable buyers. The process also helps you handle the concerns of the other three types of buyers.

For committed buyers, this means moving to Step 6, Closing the Sale.

For unconvinced buyers, this means addressing their concerns effectively and then either moving them up to Step 6 or moving them out if they've proven to be an unattainable buyer.

For not completely honest buyers, it may not be completely clear at first what you need to do. With these buyers the clarifying question (we will discuss in just a bit) you ask is key to ferreting out their real concern.

For unattainable buyers, this means thanking them for their time and moving them out of your sales pipeline.

Step 1. Listen and Clarify the Concern

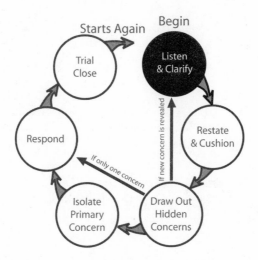

The first thing we have to do is listen. This is always great advice for a sales professional. Whenever you're in doubt about what to do, just listen. When a buyer initially expresses a concern, quickly convey that you are interested in what he is saying and show him that you understand; doing this reduces resistance.

Next, make sure you fully understand what the buyer is saying by asking *clarifying questions* (we also ask clarifying questions during discovery). Clarifying questions prompt buyers to explain what they mean or give more detail. We ask these questions for two reasons:

1. By asking clarifying questions, you can better understand your buyer's concerns so that you can effectively respond to them *later* in the process. Understanding your buyer's concerns allows you to take care of his logical needs.

2. Clarifying questions make your buyer feel better. It takes care of his emotional needs. It is human nature for us to become less agitated, annoyed, or concerned when we talk about what is bothering us (women tend to be better at this than men . . . it's a Venus and Mars thing).

> ## $500 Sales Tip!
> The more people talk about their concerns the less emotionally charged they will feel about them.
> —G.A. Bartick

Listening and asking clarifying questions makes people more receptive. Listening to understand and asking clarifying questions creates several benefits:

- We dissipate the emotion behind their concern.
- We better understand what is really concerning them.
- We reduce resistance and increase receptivity to our response.
- We find clues as to the best way to respond.
- We have more time to build our response.
- We show buyers that we are professional and emotionally mature and do not take their concern personally.
- We create a safer environment to talk honestly about other, perhaps more important concerns.

It's Not Always What You Say

One of the keys to listening is not talking. I know that sounds obvious, and it is. But why do so many sales professionals do so much talking? I think it's because we get nervous. We feel talking allows us to control the conversation and situation but, in fact, it's the one who asks the questions and listens who controls things.

$500 Sales Tip!

The one asking the questions controls
the conversation.
—G.A. Bartick

We've got to be quiet in order to listen to understand. Not only do we have to watch our mouths, but we've got to watch our body language, too. It isn't helpful to react with body language that makes you look frustrated, upset, or bored.

Here are the two things I do to listen to understand:

1. When buyers start talking about their concerns, I take a deep breath and relax. I never—and I mean absolutely never—interrupt! When we interrupt to respond or, even worse, correct buyers, we build resistance and train them to keep their concerns to themselves and not share honestly.

2. Then I follow the two-second rule: Give two seconds of silence after buyers have completed communicating their concerns. This brief pause shows your buyers you are patient and nondefensive. It also allows buyers to breathe and add additional, possibly more important information. This two-second rule is my little secret; I have not shared it with too many people. This deliberate pause, which can feel like an eternity, is one of those small things that will set you apart from your competition. When buyers voice a concern, the typical sales professional immediately responds with all the reasons why the buyers should buy.

How to Ask Clarifying Questions

Like in the Discovery step, a clarifying question prompts buyers to provide more information. Good clarifying questions can really help our buyers talk about their concerns. Here are some examples of good clarifying questions. Use the one that best fits the situation:

- *Could you tell me a little bit more about that?*
- *What exactly do you mean by that?*
- *Could you please tell me what you mean by that?*
- *Could you explain that to me in more detail?*
- *Why is that a concern?*

The key to these questions is that they are open ended (cannot be answered with a yes or no) and they encourage buyers to talk about their concerns. To get a crystal-clear understanding of a buyer's concern, you might have to ask a couple of clarifying questions. Remember, communication helps dissipate resistance and increase receptivity. Voice tone is also crucial here. You must sound inquisitive and not judgmental. If you ask the clarifying question without the right tone of voice, it can come off as condescending.

From working with thousands of sales professionals, I know that asking clarifying questions is the most difficult part of the addressing concerns process. Many sales professionals simply do not allow buyers to talk enough about what is concerning them. Consider these two examples:

Poor Example

Sales Professional: (trial close)
Julie, can you see how that will help your situation?

Buyer:
I do, but I'm kind of concerned about the price.

Sales Professional: (response)
I'm glad you brought up the price because if you really break it down and amortize the cost across the life of the web site, it only comes down to a few dollars a day. And your company is worth a few dollars a day, isn't it?

The What and the Why

Here the sales professional commits the cardinal sin of immediately re-sponding to the concern without asking clarifying questions to fully un-derstand which "cost" concern it really is (e.g., can't afford it, don't see the value in it, more expensive than the competition, etc.). He offers a rationale ("it only comes down to a few dollars a day") that may or may not address the buyer's cost concern.

Good Example

Sales Professional: (trial close)
Julie, can you see how that will help your situation?

Buyer:
I do, but I'm kind of concerned about the price.

Sales Professional: (clarifying question)
So I can understand a little better, could you tell me exactly what it is about the price that concerns you?

Buyer:
Sure. I've been looking around and have found an online service that will develop our site for less than what's in your proposal.

The What and the Why

As you can see in the poor example, the sales professional is listening to respond and jumps all over the concern before he really understands what's behind it. The net result of this type of response is a solution (in this case, amortizing the cost to realize it's only a few dollars a day) that is not at all tailored to the buyer's concern.

In the good example the sales professional is listening to understand and asks a good clarifying question to further his understanding of his buyer's concern. He is in a much better position to respond to his buyer's price concern because now he knows what the real issue is. Often buyers will label a concern under a convenient tag, such as simply saying "It costs too much" or "I can't afford that." But after asking good clarifying questions, we'll find that it is more complicated or, in some cases, a different concern altogether.

It's Not as Obvious as You Think

A lot of sales professionals say that asking clarifying questions is the most difficult part of the addressing concerns process to get used to. They say that asking clarifying questions is awkward, as if they are asking buyers to explain the obvious. But the obvious may not be as obvious as you think. For example, when my buyers tell me they are concerned about price, I really don't know *exactly* what they mean. What about our price concerns them? It could be one of a half dozen things:

- Is it just too much for them to afford?
- Is it that they can afford it, but just don't want to pay that much?
- Is our price higher than our competitor's price?
- Is it that they don't see the value and don't think our service is worth it?
- It might be that buyers are concerned only about one aspect of the pricing and think the rest is highly competitive.
- Or maybe the price is too low and they're concerned about the quality.

So it's a good idea to ask a question or two to clarify. Here are some examples of clarifying questions that help you better understand buyers' cost issues:

- *What is it specifically about the price that you are concerned about?*
- *Could you help me understand what component of the pricing you are most concerned about?*
- *Pricing can mean a lot of things. Could you help me out and explain what it is about the pricing you are most concerned about?*

With questions like these, you will get much more specific detail about the concern and, in many cases, begin to release the emotion behind the concern. It's amazing that many sales professionals don't ask clarifying questions when it is such an effective technique. Rapport is enhanced, our understanding of the situation increases, and buyers feel understood. These three important benefits will help you respond more effectively to their real concern.

Clarifying Questions Beat the Competition

When you ask clarifying questions for the first time, you might feel a little awkward. My suggestion is to push through it and watch how these simple clarifying questions, along with the two-second rule, can transform the way you address concerns. Together, the questions remove the confrontation that often accompanies many addressing concerns situations by putting you on the same side of the table as your buyer. This is the goal of the Bullet Selling addressing concerns process—to turn the entire concerns process into collaborative problem solving and to stay as far away as possible from confrontational, hardball negotiations as we can.

When Not to Ask Clarifying Questions

Clarifying questions are a great tool to further our understanding of what is really bothering buyers. However, we don't need to ask any of these questions if buyers make their concerns crystal clear in the first place.

When Not to Ask a Clarifying Question

Sales Professional: (trial close)
> *Julie, can you see how that will help your situation?*

Buyer:
> *I do, but I'm kind of concerned about the price. I've been looking around and have found an online service that will develop our site for less than what's in your proposal.*

It would be fantastic if our buyers always responded to our trial close with such a well-articulated concern, but we know from our research that this is rarely the case. What would happen if you responded to the buyer's detailed explanation with a clarifying question, such as "Could you tell me a little bit more about that?" How would Julie respond? Not too well, I would think.

Step 2. Restate and Cushion

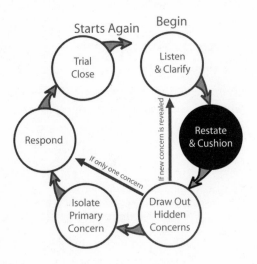

Restate What You Hear

Only after you completely understand your buyer's concern are you ready to move on to the restate and cushion step. The restate is precisely what it sounds like—no fancy jargon here. All we need to do is restate the essence of our buyer's concern in our own words. Doing so demonstrates to our buyer that we have really heard and understood what they said. Here are a few example restates:

- *What I'm hearing is that you're concerned about the fees because you're used to paying much less for this service.*
- *I understand you are concerned about all of the features on this product because you don't think you'll ever understand how to really use it.*

- *I can see how you may be nervous about getting back into the market given how big a drop your portfolio took last year before you sold out all your positions.*

- *So you're concerned that our price is $2,200 more than what you are currently paying, and the features appear to be similar.*

In the restate, it's critical to represent what buyers have said accurately. If we slant it, spin it, or slightly modify it for any reason, we are taking a big risk with our credibility and rapport. We will get better results if we think of ourselves as reporters who accurately distill what has been said into a simple summary statement that buyers will agree with 100%.

Cushioning the Restate

After listening to concerns and using clarifying questions, it's natural to feel the urge to respond defensively because, let's face it, it often stings a little. The concern might sound like a personal attack on you, your company, your work, or your product.

When buyers sense that you're getting defensive, the conversation is negatively affected. This is where the cushion comes in. A cushion is a nonthreatening way of reacting to unpleasant news that allows the conversation to remain cooperative and nonconfrontational. Cushions are simple phrases such as:

- *I hear what you're saying.*
- *That's a valid point you're making.*
- *I understand what you're telling me, and it's important.*
- *Thank you for helping me understand how you see the situation.*
- *Thank you, now I understand your concern better.*
- *I can appreciate that.*

When you put a solid restate together with a nondefensive cushion, five positive things happen:

1. You don't add unnecessary friction to the conversation.

2. You show buyers that you are truly listening to what they are saying.

3. You convey to buyers that their opinions and responses are important to you.

4. You demonstrate that you are not defensive and that it is safe to tell you the truth.

5. You give yourself a moment to take a deep breath, collect your thoughts, and avoid the immediate urge to respond to their concern.

By now, you can probably see that the addressing concerns process is similar to discovery in two very important ways. First, we ask clarifying questions and second, we summarize when we feel we have a good understanding of the situation. In both steps it's important to ask enough clarifying questions to gain a thorough understanding and create an emotional connection with buyers. It's the "listened to" and "understood" parts that soften buyers' resistance.

Step 3. Draw Out Hidden Concerns

So what do 90% of sales professionals do after they've heard a concern, asked clarifying questions, and restated and cushioned? According to our research, the vast majority feel compelled to respond to the concern. It typically goes something like this:

Poor Example

Sales Professional: (trial close)
> Well, Ms. Jones, now that we've had a chance to talk about your insurance situation and the ABC agency in more detail, can you see how this coverage will protect your home?

Buyer:
> You've made it all very clear, but I'm concerned about the fact that your firm isn't really very well known.

Sales Professional: (clarifying question)
> Thank you for being so honest. Could you help me understand a little bit more what you mean by that?

Buyer:
> Sure, my brother had his health insurance with a small company, I forget the name, but when his wife got cancer they had to pay tens of thousands of dollars in medical bills that the insurance company would not cover. I'm kind of scared of going with a small company because I don't want the same thing to happen to my family.

Sales Professional: (restate)
> It sounds to me like you want to make sure you're insured with a reputable insurance company so that you can rest easy knowing you're adequately covered if your family has a medical emergency.

Sales Professional: (cushion)
> I can certainly understand why that would be a concern of yours.

Sales Professional: (response)
> I'm glad you brought that up, Ms. Jones. Let me tell you a little more about the history of ABC Agency. We've been in the insurance market for over 50 years...

The What and the Why

In this example the sales professional did ask the clarifying questions and even restated and cushioned. Then came the rookie mistake, jumping on the first concern he heard. And after observing thousands of sales professionals in action, we can state unequivocally that this is exactly what most do. But there is a better way. Compare what you just read with the next example, which illustrates drawing out hidden concerns.

Good Example

Sales Professional: (trial close)
> Well, Ms. Jones, now that we've had a chance to talk about your insurance situation and the ABC agency in more detail, can you see how this coverage will protect your family?

Buyer:
> You've made it all very clear, but I'm concerned about the fact that your firm isn't really very well known.

Sales Professional: (clarifying question)
> Thank you for being so honest. Could you help me understand a little bit more what you mean by that?

Buyer:
> Sure, my brother had his health insurance with a small company, I forget the name, but when his wife got cancer they had to pay tens of thousands of dollars in medical bills that the insurance company would not cover. I'm kind of scared of going with a small company because I don't want the same thing to happen to my family.

Sales Professional: (restate)
> It sounds to me like your concern is that you want to make sure you're insured with a reputable insurance company so that you can rest easy knowing you're adequately covered if your family has a medical emergency.

Sales Professional: (cushion)
> I can certainly understand why that would be a concern of yours.

Sales Professional: (draw out additional concerns)
> In addition to that, do you have any other concerns you could share with me?

The What and the Why

This last sentence makes such a difference. By asking if there are any other concerns, the sales professional has continued the cooperative nature of the call and is encouraging the buyer to openly share any other concerns he may have. Many times when I teach the drawing out additional concerns step, participants say to me, "Hold on a second, G.A. You're telling me to ask the buyer for more concerns? What if they have 17 concerns?" What if they do? You have to address them all. Even if you do a great job of addressing 16 concerns, you may not get the sale because you didn't even know about the 17th concern.

Sales professionals who draw out all the concerns are reacting in a thoroughly nonconfrontational manner, which generates a greater sense of cooperation and rapport. It's not about "proving" you're right; it's about creating a cooperative situation through communication where rapport increases and buyer resistance drops.

Here are some example questions for drawing out hidden concerns.

- *In addition to the cost, is there anything else?*
- *Are there any other concerns you have?*
- *Can you think of anything else that is causing you concern?*
- *Is there anything else we've discussed that you feel concerned about?*

And my personal favorite:

- *In addition to that, is there anything else?*

For maximum impact, phrase this question in an open and curious way. The key to uncovering hidden concerns is to invite buyers to share. It's about turning off the "concerns are a pain in my neck" mentality that seems so prevalent in most of us, and turning on the "I really want to know what you're thinking because I want to help you" state of mind. Use this process and get all of the concerns out in the open before you even think about responding to any of them.

Cast a Net, Not a Line

As we mentioned before, drawing out additional concerns is sort of like fishing. Most sales professionals use a single line approach to catch only one concern from the sea of concerns. Our research shows us that top performers use a net approach. Instead of being concerned with catching just one fish, top performers throw out their nets and troll around until they are able to scoop up all the concerns. That way they get a much clearer picture of what's going on under the surface.

If You Ask, You Shall Receive

If you use this draw-out process, you'll find that buyers will share more concerns about half the time. When they express another concern, go right back to the listen and clarify step at the top of the Bullet Selling addressing concerns process. Then restate and cushion and draw out more hidden concerns *until the buyer says he has no more concerns to share.* I have to admit, doing this takes a lot of patience. It's much easier to hear a concern and immediately respond to it, but you will not close nearly as many sales as the sales professional who draws out all of the buyer's concerns before responding to any of them.

Step 4. Isolate the Primary Concern

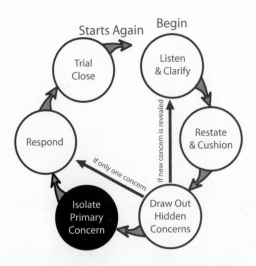

From our research the typical buyer shares about 1.4 concerns per sale, so you don't have to worry about the drawing out step taking too much time. You'll be able to haul all of their concerns into the net within a minute or two. The next step is to determine which concern to address first. The vast majority of sales professionals respond to the first concern the buyer mentioned. Unfortunately, according to our research, this is the most important concern only about half the time. That's another reason why it's important to have buyers reveal all of their concerns before you respond to any of them.

Instead of Assuming, Ask

The best way to isolate which concern is the primary concern is to ask. Here are a few examples of isolating questions that we've culled from our research.

- *Which concern would you like to talk about first?*
- *Of the two concerns you shared with me, which one is weighing most heavily on your mind?*
- *Of the two you mentioned, which is your primary concern?*

When you ask questions like these, buyers typically pause a moment and then tell you the concern that is most important to them. The key is to let buyers tell you where to start instead of assuming. Every once in a while a buyer will say that all of the issues are equally important. Ask these folks, "Which of these concerns would you like to talk about first?" This will at least give you a starting point.

Successful people typically have a knack for spending the bulk of their time on "important" things. Human beings intuitively sense that people who spend their time on high-priority activities are somehow more successful, more trustworthy, and more credible. Therefore, when we isolate the primary concern, we are telling our buyers that we want to spend our time on what's most important to them, and this reflects positively on us. It may seem like a small point (and it is), but being successful in sales is really about doing a lot of little things a little bit better than the competition. It's not about having one big knockout punch in the closing moments of the sale.

Putting the First Four Steps Together

Sales Professional: (trial close)
> *Should we go ahead and get these speakers so you can watch a DVD in surround sound tonight?*

Buyer:
> *Well, I'm not quite sure. I've had a bad experience with wireless speakers before and I'm afraid they just won't work.*

Sales Professional: (clarifying question)
> *Can you tell me what happened?*

Buyer:
> *About two years ago I bought this new state-of-the-art wireless stereo system for my girlfriend and it just didn't deliver the power we were looking for.*

Sales Professional: (clarifying question)
> *I see. What about the stereo wasn't powerful enough?*

Buyer:
> *It was mostly the bass. It was all washed out and distorted.*

Sales Professional: (restate and cushion)
> *So as I understand it, you're concerned because you've had a pair of wireless speakers before and their performance was disappointing, especially the bass. That's a reasonable concern.*

(continued)

Sales Professional: (draw out hidden concerns)
> *Is there anything else that is a concern to you?*

Buyer:
> *In fact, there is. I'm not really that good with electronics.*

Sales Professional: (clarifying question)
> *Tell me a little about that.*

Buyer:
> *Well, I'm afraid I won't be able to install them correctly.*

Sales Professional: (restate & cushion)
> *So you're a little concerned that you might not be able to install the system. I totally understand.*

Sales Professional: (draw out hidden concerns)
> *In addition to that, is there anything else?*

Buyer:
> *No. That's it.*

Sales Professional: (isolate the primary concern)
> *So between your concern that the speakers won't sound great and your concern about installing them, which would you say concerns you the most?*

Buyer:
> *I'd say it's the quality of the sound.*

Sales Professional: (respond)
> ***(Stay tuned...that's coming in the next chapter!)***

Click Here!

Log on to www.silverbulletselling.com to listen to this in action and to see more examples.

CHAPTER TWENTY-THREE

Responding to Concerns

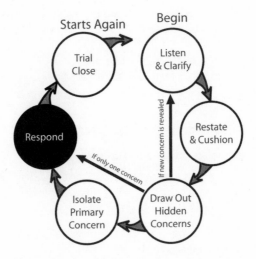

Responding effectively to concerns requires you to become skilled in two areas:

1. Identifying the concern(s)

2. Responding to the concern(s)

In Chapter 22 we learned how to identify concerns by using the first four steps of the addressing concerns process:

1. Listen and clarify

2. Restate and cushion

3. Draw out hidden concerns (go back through steps 2–4 if buyers express more concerns)

4. Isolate the primary concern

Our research shows that when sales professionals become accomplished at these steps, they are rewarded with a dramatic increase in their closing percentage.

Now it's time to take a close look at step 5 of the addressing concerns process—responding to concerns. This is the second skill set you must master to respond effectively to concerns.

The concerns are all on the table in front of you and you know which is the most important. Now all you have to do is respond in such a way that will satisfy the concerns and allow you to close the sale. Stay cool. Stay calm. Stay collected. It's a big job, but we're going to give you the tools you need.

Three Ways to Respond to the Cost Concern

After reviewing our research we recognized that sales professionals utilize three different strategies to respond to the cost concern:

1. Increase the perceived value of your product/service so buyers are more motivated to buy

2. Decrease the price of the product/service so it is a better value

3. Argue with buyers about price

Strategy #1: Increase the Perceived Value of Your Product/Service

This is far and away the most desirable strategy because when we increase perceived value, everybody wins. Sales professionals win because they get to complete a sale at full price and buyers win because they get the product or service they value so much.

A simple example of this strategy in action would be if I were to offer to sell you a $20 bill for $30. First you'd look at me kind of cockeyed to make sure I was serious. Then you'd look the note over. Chances are you'd say, "What are you, nuts? I'm not going to pay you $30 for a $20 bill."

But what if I then presented a certificate of authenticity from Smythe, one of the world's most reputable numismatic companies, guaranteeing that this 1969 B Series $20 bill (Serial Number: G00684077) is worth $150? Then what would you think? You'd think it was still ridiculous, only this time in your favor.

What's interesting here is that the bill did not change, but your *perception* of its value changed. Now you probably see the $20 bill as a bargain instead of a rip-off. You can apply this same principle to *any* product or service for sale, from the most complex billion-dollar negotiation to candy in a gumball machine. When you improve the perceived value of what you're selling, the sale comes much easier.

The Bullet Selling Process Builds Perceived Value Throughout

The entire Bullet Selling process is built around maximizing the perceived value of you and the product/service you sell. For example, in the Building Rapport step, your agenda statement and credibility statement build your perceived value. During the Discovery step, the smart questions you ask do the same thing. (Even mind mapping reflects well on you.) In the Tailored Solution step, your business philosophy, competitive advantage, and solution increase your perceived value, and the link feature bridge benefit statements (LFBBs) of your products/services also raise their perceived value.

What Is Perceived Value Anyway?

To understand how to increase perceived value, it's important to first understand what value really is. According to our research, perceived value can be influenced by 10 things:

1. Perceived value is subjective. What's valuable to you isn't necessarily valuable to others.
2. Perceived value is directly tied to wants and needs. (Things that we want or need have high perceived value.)

3. Perceived value is often influenced by those around us and by advertising.

4. Perceived value can change quickly. Products and services can go in and out of style.

5. Most people are motivated to buy when the perceived value exceeds what they view as the price.

6. Perceived value can be influenced by who is doing the selling. Sales professionals with skill usually can sell products/services at a premium price.

7. Often the perceived value of a product/service is compromised simply because buyers don't fully understand all of the features and benefits.

8. The reputation of the company offering the product/service influences perceived value. The impact of a "brand" is enormous.

9. Value perception is also influenced by the way you express yourself—the way you dress, the way you communicate, the way you carry yourself. Professionalism typically builds value.

10. Perceived value begins to build (or shrink) with the very first contact you have with the buyer. Every conversation, e-mail, voice message, phone call, meeting, and interaction will put another brick into (or take another brick away from) the foundation of the overall value perception.

As you can see, many of these factors happen well before the point in the sales process where concerns come up. By becoming proficient at the Bullet Selling process, you will proactively build perceived value in yourself and your products/services. Now let's focus on how we can respond in a way that will raise the value perception in our buyers' minds.

Artillery for Building Value

Two techniques can help you build perceived value to overcome cost concerns:

1. Tailoring a response
2. Using evidence

Building Value by Tailoring Your Response to the Concern

The first thing to do is tailor a response to your buyer's concern. This means using all the appropriate tools in the Silver Bullet Selling ammo pouch, including:

- Credibility statement
- LFBBs of your products and services
- Business philosophy
- Competitive advantage

We deliver the response using two elements:

1. Transition with a restate and cushion
2. Response

If a buyer's concern is "paying too much money for your product or service," your response might sound something like this:

Food Industry

Respond with Business Philosophy:

We built our business on value, and that's why we offer a complete 100% money-back guarantee. We take the risk factor out of the deal for our customers and put it squarely on our shoulders. If you are not completely satisfied with the food we provide, or if you feel it's not a good value, we will refund all of your money. No questions asked.

If you choose to respond using LFBBs, your response might sound like this:

Food Industry

Respond with LFBBs:

We've been delivering meals to families' doorsteps for more than 30 years. **(Link)** *And you talked about how important serving wholesome food is to you, and that's why* **(Feature)** *we sell only USDA certified organic meats and produce, and we cut out the supermarket middlemen* **(Bridge)**, *which is great for you because* **(Benefit)** *our prices are lower and we pass the savings along to our customers. You'd pay at least 15% more at the supermarket and you can use the extra money to join the fitness club you talked about earlier.*

Or, if you include both in your response, it would sound like this:

Food Industry

Respond with LFBBs and Business Philosophy:

We've been delivering meals to families' doorsteps for more than 30 years. And you talked about how important serving wholesome food is to you, and that's why we sell only USDA certified organic meats and produce. And because we cut out the supermarket middlemen, our costs are lower and we pass the savings along to our buyers. You'd pay at least 15% more at the supermarket.

It's important that you know we built our business on quality and value. That's why we offer a complete 100% money-back guarantee. We take the risk out of the deal for our customers and put it squarely on our shoulders. If you are not completely satisfied with the food we provide, or if you feel it's not a good value, we'll refund all of your money. No questions asked.

Click Here!

Want to see more industry-specific examples? Go to
www.silverbulletselling.com.

The more features and benefits you know, the more clearly you understand all your competitive advantages and the more prepared you'll be to handle cost concerns. This is just another reason why sales professionals need to build their Reserve Power.

Building Value by Using Evidence

Top performers have told us that the addressing concerns process is most effective when they tie down their responses with evidence. Evidence is anything you can use to substantiate what you say; it's the proof that will transform what you say into indisputable fact. As we covered in Chapter 20, evidence can come in many forms:

- Brochures
- Newspaper and magazine articles
- Studies
- Charts and tables
- Testimonials
- Buyer success stories

When used properly, evidence is an incredibly useful bullet to have in your ammo pouch. Sharing a testimonial that addresses a buyer's cost concern is a nonthreatening way to allow a third-party opinion into the conversation. For instance, if a buyer were to say, "I think the fees your firm charges for trading are absolutely too high. I can trade with Discount Brokerage for $12 a trade." Here's what your response might sound like:

Financial Industry

Testimonial:

(Pull out highlighted letter to show buyer)

As you can see here in the first paragraph, Mrs. Sklar describes how she used to trade at Discount Brokerage and enjoyed the low commission fees on transactions. She goes on to explain that a number of the transactions she made ended up losing thousands of dollars. Here in the second paragraph she explains how the complete portfolio analysis and asset allocation we worked on together resulted in a completely different set of equities. And here in the final paragraph she talks about how much better her portfolio has performed since she's been with us and that the cost of the transactions is insignificant compared to the quality of the advice and overall asset management services she now receives.

And that's what's really at the core of our message to you. The performance of your portfolio is what really matters. That is what will determine how quickly and steadily your retirement assets grow and enable you to have enough money to retire at 62 like you want.

 Click Here!

You know where to see more examples…
www.silverbulletselling.com.

As you can see from the example, third-party evidence can be very powerful when it addresses the buyer's concern head on. During the Tailored Solution step, we worked on creating influential testimonials, and that work will pay off for you here. (Just remember to bring relevant testimonials with you to a call. Maybe you should add "Bring testimonials" to your pre-call planning checklist.)

While we're talking about evidence, give some thought to what forms of evidence would be appropriate for your sales. Another effective strategy is sharing a story about a buyer who overcame the same concern by using your product/service. The key to telling an effective buyer success story is to develop a little empathy with the buyer by showing that others have felt the same way.

Printing Industry

Success Story:

> **(Issue)** *We work with the 14 offices of Thompson Realty and they're constantly ordering big print jobs of flyers with very tight deadlines. What they've found is that we are able to meet their deadlines, even when other printers had let them down.* **(Resolution)** *They love that we're open 24/7 because* **(Benefit)** *they know if a house falls out of escrow, they can call us at 6:00 PM and we'll have a team working all night so they can have flyers and signage and other promotional materials ready by 8:00 the next morning. It's that "always ready" mentality that makes the difference.*

Strategy #2: Negotiating the Price

We've covered in detail the strategy of increasing perceived value as the preferred way of handling cost concerns. However, many sales professionals aren't skilled enough to increase perceived value, so they resort to dropping the price to overcome buyers' concerns. In most cases these people do a poor job of executing the first four steps of the sales process. When we don't do a great job in discovery or at presenting a tailored solution, it is much more difficult to be successful at handling concerns because the perceived value of the product or service is so low. That's why so many sales professionals choose to minimize the importance of the concerns by immediately lowering the price and accepting the unresolved concerns as part of the deal. Discount pricing typically sets up a precedent and cost, not value, becomes the driving force of the relationship. This result is not compatible with the goals of the Bullet Selling process which strives to create a different and unique buying experience and, as a result, loyal, long-term relationships with buyers.

Negotiating by Building Value

I am asked often to develop and deliver a program on negotiating. I have read many books and even attended seminars on this subject. The one universal tidbit I keep hearing is "Once an offer has been made, the one who speaks first loses." Basically this means: State your point and then shut up. I guess during that silence something magical is supposed to happen. The calm quietness is supposed to penetrate your buyers' psyches and bring them into agreement with your solution. Maybe I'm not waiting long enough, or maybe I'm missing something completely, but I do think there is more to negotiating than waiting for the other guy to talk.

Negotiations can be about terms, conditions, or, most commonly, price. In order to win a negotiation you have to know your buyers. You have to know their current situation and their desired situation. You need to know why they need your solution and how it's going to improve their world.

Often, sales professionals lower their prices without any negotiation. This is a fatal mistake. If you move off your position immediately, you've diminished the value of your product or service.

I was recently in a negotiation with a potential buyer. He stated that our daily fee was quite a bit higher than that of another company he was considering and asked me to bring my price down. At this point I had several choices. I could:

1. Ask "What is the daily rate of the competition?"
2. Make a counteroffer with a reduced price
3. Build the value of my solution by revisiting what I learned during my thorough discovery step

I chose the latter.

I told my buyer, "You mentioned how important this program is going to be in helping your organization increase results by becoming better at team selling and asking for referrals from your current clients. And getting a team of 240 sales professionals to do that is not an easy task. We've had success with other retail organizations where we have been able to do just that. That is why we charge what we believe is a fair price, and you'll more than make it up on your return on investment." Then I simply gave a trial close: "Does that make sense?"

This is always my first response. But what if my buyer still says our price is too high? Then I may need to go to a fallback or counteroffer, perhaps offering fewer training days.

Other Negotiating Principles

In many industries such as real estate and law, negotiation is a common and accepted practice. In their classic book *Getting to Yes: Negotiating Agreement without Giving In*, Roger Fisher and William Ury describe their four principles for effective, principled negotiation:

1. Separate the people from the problem.

   During negotiations people tend to become personally involved with the issues and with their side's positions. Often they take responses to those issues and positions as personal attacks. Separating the people from the issues allows the parties to address the issues without damaging their relationship. It also helps them get a clearer view of the substantive problem.

2. Focus on interests rather than positions.

   Good agreements focus on the parties' interests rather than their positions. As Fisher and Ury explain, "Your position is something you have decided upon. Your interests are what caused you to so decide." Defining a problem in terms of positions means that at least one party will "lose" the dispute. Defining a problem in terms of the parties' underlying interests often makes it easier to find a solution that satisfies both parties' interests.

3. Generate a variety of options.

   The negotiating parties should come together informally to brainstorm all possible solutions to the problem. Only after a variety of ideas have been made should the group begin evaluating them. Evaluation should start with the most promising ideas and the parties should also refine and improve the ideas at this point.

4. Insist that the agreement be based on objective criteria.

When interests are directly opposed, the negotiating parties should use objective criteria to resolve their differences. The parties must agree on which criterion is best for their situation. One way to test for objectivity is to ask if both sides would agree to be bound by those standards. Decisions based on reasonable standards make it easier for the parties to agree and preserve their good relationship.

Strategy #3: Argue with the Buyer

Arguing is for brothers, not for buyers. Avoid it at all costs.

Addressing Concerns Other than Cost

The List of Eight identifies the eight most common types of concerns:

1. Cost
2. Terms and conditions
3. I don't need it
4. I have to think about it
5. I don't want to go through the hassle of changing
6. Sales professional's lack of experience
7. I have to talk to my colleague/boss/spouse
8. I had a previous bad experience

So far we've covered the cost concern. What about the other seven? The good news is that some of the value-building and negotiating techniques we've already covered effectively handle four of the remaining seven concerns. Let's look at each concern and determine a strategy to handle it effectively.

Terms and Conditions

Sometimes buyers will raise a concern about one or more of the terms and conditions. The most effective way to handle these types of concerns is to use clarifying questions until you thoroughly understand the buyers' concerns. Then you isolate each concern and negotiate it separately.

I Don't Need It

I Have to Think about It

I Don't Want to Go through the Hassle of Changing

Buyers raise these three concerns when the perceived value of your product/service isn't high enough. Therefore, it makes sense to handle these concerns by raising perceived value through evidence (e.g., testimonials, buyer success stories, newspaper articles, studies, charts and tables, brochures).

Sales Professional's Lack of Experience

Sales professionals who are relatively new to the job often have to handle this concern. From our research we've learned that top performers address this issue with a lot of success stories and testimonials. Another method is aligning themselves with more experienced and successful colleagues who go out on sales calls with them to make the initial sale.

I Have to Talk to My Colleague/Boss/Spouse

Sometimes buyers give this concern when the concern is really their own (and sometimes not). This is my favorite concern to handle. When buyers say they have to talk to someone else, I empathetically respond,

"I completely understand. What might your (colleague/boss/spouse) object to?" Most of the time they say," They are going to be concerned about the price." That's when I know I need to address the price concern.

The "I have to talk to my colleague/boss/spouse" concern is usually a smoke screen. Do not get faked out by it. Every time you hear this concern, ask the simple clarifying question: "What do you think they would object to?" And watch it come back to price. If you can do this effectively, the original concern about having to discuss this with someone else often goes away.

I Had a Previous Bad Experience

The first thing top performers do when buyers mention a previous bad experience is ask buyers to explain in detail what happened, then they take full responsibility for the issue and apologize. It doesn't matter that it wasn't their fault. After the apology they explain why things are different and how they will make sure the problem will not happen again. If you're going to use this strategy, you have to be willing to make good on your promise.

Trial Close

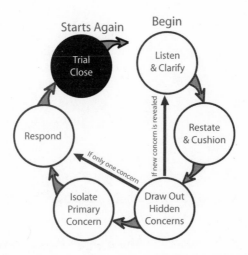

You have responded to your buyer's concerns by tailoring a response and/or using evidence. How effective was your response? The only way to know is to test it with a trial close. Here are some examples:

- *Knowing all that, do you understand why that is a fair price?*
- *Do you feel better knowing that we've worked with customers who had the same concerns as you?*
- *Does that help explain why we're the best option for you?*
- *Does that make sense?*

If you were successful at satisfying your buyer's concern, move on to:

1. Handle concern #2 by repeating the same process, or
2. The Closing the Sale step (Chapter 25)

However, if your buyer is still not quite convinced, one of three things is going on:

1. You did not completely understand his concern. In this case you need to fall back to step 1 of the addressing concerns process and ask some more clarifying questions.
2. You did not do an adequate job of responding to your buyer's concern. If this is the situation, you are in a vulnerable position. Your only choice is to fall back to step 5 of the addressing concerns process. Try to respond to the concern more effectively by negotiating the terms or price, and if you are unsuccessful, know when it is time give up, thank the buyer for his time, and move on.
3. You did a fine job of understanding and responding to your buyer's concern, but he just isn't interested. In this situation, you can try

to reduce the price or just graciously give up the sale and thank the buyer for his time.

☞ READY, AIM, FIRE!

Build Your Own Response

The beautiful thing about concerns is that they are predictable in two ways. First, we know that almost every buyer is going to have them. Second, we already know the list of concerns they are going to raise. Armed with this understanding, top sales professionals prepare by developing responses to specific concerns before they ever come up.

The best responses are customized to the actual concerns you hear every day. Go ahead and use the questions below to help you create customized responses to the concerns you hear most often. You can write your answers on a separate sheet of paper, or you can use the worksheet at www.silverbulletselling.com. Before you begin this exercise, it would be helpful to think of an upcoming meeting and prepare responses to the concerns you think your buyer might have.

Click Here!
Go to silverbulletselling.com to find worksheets you can print out and write on.

State the Concern: _____

- What clarifying question would you ask?
- How might your buyer respond to your clarifying question? What would he say?
- What strategy are you going to use to respond to the concern?
- What response would you give to overcome this concern?
- What trial close will you use?

☛ READY, AIM, FIRE!

Practice Delivering Your Own Responses

If you think you can handle your buyer's concerns effectively without practicing, you should be the one writing this book. This is where I practice the most because when a buyer is challenging my value and the value of my services, the pressure's on.

1. Stand up with your responses in hand.
2. Read your responses aloud twice verbatim, including the steps of the process.
3. Read your responses four to six times slowly until you begin to memorize the process (not the words, but the steps of the process).
4. Practice saying your responses one at a time until you have the process memorized and can communicate it without your notes.
5. Take a break.
6. Repeat steps 3 and 4 until your delivery is smooth and uncanned.
7. Using a tape recorder, record your delivery to hear what you sound like. Assess what you hear and adjust your delivery until you are very satisfied. Make sure your tone of voice is enthusiastic, not defensive.

Remember that you can't win them all, but you can win more when you use an effective process and execute it well.

Using the Addressing Concerns Process at Home

I've been speaking and teaching the Bullet Selling process all over the world for the past 11 years. During that time my wife has not once heard me speak, deliver a keynote, or teach a class. Why not? Because then she would know the process and all my secrets. I tell you, Bullet Selling is not just for the workplace.

I was working in Jacksonville, Florida, Tuesday through Friday for many months. I would fly out on Monday and return home on Friday night. On the return flight, during a short layover at the Dallas/Fort Worth Airport, I'd phone home to say good night to the kids and talk to Kelly.

There I was at the Dallas/Fort Worth airport on a Friday night, and I made my call. Now realize the fate of my entire weekend was often predicated on the outcome of this call. Kelly answered and from her voice I could tell something was up. So I asked, "Honey, is something up?"

"Well, yes. I'm a little upset at your daughter Alicia." (All of a sudden she is *my* daughter.)

"Why is that?" So far, so good.

"Well, you know, she has a piano recital this weekend, and when she got home from school yesterday and today she went straight down to Serena's house and did not practice."

Then I said, "Why did you let Alicia go over to Serena's? You know you can't let her go play before she practices piano!" There was a long silence on the other end of the phone, and I could tell that I had just ruined my weekend.

When I returned to Jacksonville the following week, my class asked how my weekend was. I explained what had happened, and they quickly reminded me of the process. All week they practiced with me making my phone call from Dallas and using the process.

On Friday night I'm in Dallas and I make the phone call. Again I can tell something's up. I ask, "Honey, is there anything I should know about?"

"Yes. I'm a little perturbed with Carly."

"Why's that?" (Great clarifying question.)

"Because when she came home yesterday from school, she and Jack played PlayStation until she had to go to dance class. So we were up until almost 10:00 doing her homework."

Moment of truth. I can respond and try to solve my wife's problem, or I can continue with the next step of the process: restate and cushion.

"So you're upset with Carly because she did not get her homework done before dance. I can totally understand your frustration." Then I caught her by surprise when I added, "In addition to that, is there anything else?" (Folks, there always is!)

"Yes there is. I had to spend my entire morning today picking up after your kids before the housekeeper came."

Now, this cleaning the house before the house is cleaned is something I just don't understand, but I hear it is a national phenomenon.

"So, you had to pick up the house for the maid. I can see how frustrating that would be." There was my restate and cushion. What's next? I need to continue to draw out additional concerns. "Is there anything else?"

"Well, hon, when you leave on Monday morning can you please put your cereal bowl in the dishwasher? This is not the Hilton."

"I can certainly do that. Is there anything else?"

"No, honey." Now I need to isolate the primary concern.

"So what would you like to talk about first?"

"How about Carly and the PlayStation?"

"Great. How can I help?"

"When I talk to Carly about getting her homework done before she goes to dance, you have to back me up."

"I can do that. Anything else I can do?"

"No. I can't wait for you to get home. I love you."

It was sizzling in the Bartick household that weekend!

So there you have it. If you want to develop relationships that are trusting and supportive, where resistance is low and receptivity is high, you need to listen and clarify, then restate and cushion the problems, frustrations, and concerns the people around you have before you try to fix them. In fact, resist the temptation to fix and listen instead. You'll be amazed at how capable the people around you are at solving their problems—and loving you—if you simply become a better, more curious and understanding listener.

CHAPTER TWENTY-FOUR

Vaccinating the Buyer against the Competition

It happens all the time. After you effectively handle all of your buyers' concerns, they throw another obstacle at you.

"G.A., the presentation was excellent. You obviously understand the problems that are confronting us, and we like the recommendations you've made. Because this is such an important decision for us, we are considering proposals from other consulting companies. The next step is to meet with everyone over the next two weeks, and then we'll make a decision."

This is music to my ears and the reason I always like to present my proposal first. Many books and sales gurus talk about how important it is to present your proposal last. I say go first! I want to be the one that sets the bar high and have all my competition be compared to me. If you are not first, sometimes the decision is made before buyers even get to you. Going first also gives me the opportunity to vaccinate buyers against the competition by telling them what questions to ask of the competing companies. During my pre-call planning I develop some questions that will point out my strengths compared to my competition.

In order to vaccinate buyers against the competition, follow these three steps:

1. Advise your buyers that it's good to shop around and choose the best provider.

Yes, I am telling you it is okay to tell your buyers to shop around. Even if they don't come out and say "We're going to look at a few other solutions," assume they are. So get out in front of this and take a strong position by using the vaccinating process.

2. Give your buyers a few questions to ask the competition.

Look at your company, your products, and your competitive advantages over the competition. Arm your buyers with these competitive advantages in the form of questions they can ask your competition.

3. Answer the questions.

Then you need to give your buyers answers to the questions.

I have used this process many times and have had buyers later call me up and say, "You know, G.A., you were right. The other company we were talking to does not customize their programs."

Here's what a vaccination I might deliver to a pharmaceutical company might sound like:

Vaccinating the Buyer against the Competition

(Advise to shop)
I think you're wise to do your due diligence and check out other consulting companies. While you're at it, you might consider asking them a few questions:

(Provide questions)
1. *Have any of their top officers worked as executives in the pharmaceutical industry?*
2. *What kind of success have they had working with pharmaceutical companies?*
3. *Do they 100% guarantee their work?*

(Answer the questions)
I'm not sure if you're aware that one of our consultants was an EVP over at Merck. He brings 10 years of experience in the pharmaceutical industry to the table. We use his insights to create solutions for our pharmaceutical partners and have had a very strong string of success. In fact, over the past three years we've worked with more than a half dozen pharmaceutical companies and have increased sales by more than 37% in each division we've trained. We're so certain that our process works that we unconditionally guarantee our work.

READY, AIM, FIRE!

Build Your Own Vaccination

 ## Click Here!
Go to silverbulletselling.com to find Vaccinating the Buyer worksheets you can print out for free.

Tips on Addressing Concerns

1. Remember that concerns are a natural part of the Bullet Selling process. They are not necessarily an indication that buyers do not want to buy from you.

2. Making decisions creates anxiety for many people. Often these concerns are verbally expressed emotional hesitation. Allow your buyers to talk about their concerns, and watch their resistance drop.

3. Listening is the key to addressing concerns. Put at least as much effort into listening to and clarifying your buyers' concerns as you do into how you respond to them.

4. Restate and cushion every concern before you respond. Show buyers you have heard their concerns and that you know they are important to them.

5. When addressing concerns, express a genuine interest to help your buyers. This will prevent you from responding defensively.

6. Never argue with buyers. Instead, focus your attention on increasing the perceived value of yourself, your products, and your services.

7. Don't respond to the first concern until you have drawn out all of the hidden concerns. Often the buyers' first concern is not their most important concern.

8. When buyers have more than one concern, ask them to tell you which concern is the most important and begin there.

9. Think about various forms of evidence you could use for specific concerns.

10. When you respond to buyers' concerns, maintain a consultative, nonadversarial approach.

Closing the Sale

1. Pre-Call Planning
2. Building Rapport
3. Discovery
4. Tailored Solution
5. Addressing Concerns
6. Closing the Sale

CHAPTER TWENTY-FIVE

Closing the Sale Overview

If you don't A-S-K, then you don't G-E-T.

—G.A. Bartick

Closing the Sale Defined

Q: What is closing?

A: Closing is the natural conclusion of the 6-Step Bullet Selling process and refers to completing the final details of the sale and setting expectations for the future. This is why we say closing the deal is opening a relationship.

Q: Why is closing so important?

A: Because closing sales is what sales professionals are paid good money to do!

> ### Did you know...
> *Glengarry Glen Ross* is also a 1984 Pulitzer Prize and Tony award winning play by David Mamet. The play draws from Mamet's stint as a typist in a Chicago real estate office in the late 1960s.

"Coffee's for closers" is the famous fire-up speech that Blake (played by Alec Baldwin) delivers to his sales team in the classic movie *Glengarry Glen Ross*. In less than two minutes Blake spells out every unsavory stereotype about sales professionals. The film, set in Chicago, portrays a collection of unmotivated real estate brokers who use every underhanded, manipulative, dishonest trick to persuade unwilling buyers to purchase undesirable real estate.

In the movie, Blake, a VP of Sales, shows up to motivate his troops. In his speech (check it out on YouTube) he tells them how it all comes down to closing. "A. B. C. Always. Be. Closing," he screams. "Only one thing counts in life. Get them to sign on the line that is dotted. If you can't close, go hit the BRICKS!!!"

When I saw the movie I cringed at being associated with those characters. However, I do agree with some of the things Blake said. Let's start with the idea that we should always be closing. I couldn't agree with him more. Closing starts with the Pre-Call Planning step of the Bullet Selling process and continues all the way through Step 6, Closing the Sale.

But this is where my agreement stops. I take umbrage at Blake's closing tactics. He believes that closing is a skill, one that separates the real pros—the sales professionals who make the real money—from those who don't. My research tells me that closing is not a single skill, but a process. The sale happens only after courting and building a trusting relationship with buyers, whether the courtship takes five minutes or five years. The entire Bullet Selling process is designed to culminate with the Closing the Sale step. If you blow one of the first five steps, no high-powered closing technique or one-liner will save you. Understand that closing, when done properly, is the natural next step of the process, and actually opens the door to a satisfied buyer who will want to do more business with you and refer business to you as well.

Could You Be Better. . .

At closing the sale?

Could you be better at . . .

Y N   Asking for the order?

Y N   Managing the details after the close?

Y N   Managing the expectations of your buyer after the close?

Y N   Exceeding your buyer's expectations?

Y N   Closing more sales?

A Bullet from G.A.'s Chamber

I had been working with CPS Insurance in Irvine, California, for several years when Andy Holden, the CEO and President, asked if I could put together a four-hour customized advanced closing technique workshop for his 100 top performers. I thought about it for several moments. The first thing that came into my head was "Here's an opportunity for a sale. Jump on it!" But then my better judgment took over and I told him, "Thanks Andy, I'd love to do it. My advanced closing technique workshop lasts about five minutes and all we do during the session is practice the mantra 'If you don't A-S-K, then you don't G-E-T.'"

The truth is that sales professional who close more sales do make more money, but the question is: Why do they close more sales? Is it because they're good at closing, or is it that closing happens more often with these sales professionals because of all the other things they do well during the sales process? Thirty-six thousand pages of notes and 6,000 interviews tell me it's the latter. I acknowledge that in today's world there are still some industries (flea market selling certainly qualifies) where a relentless closing attack really works, but there are many more industries where hardball closing is the quickest way to the loser's bracket.

CHAPTER TWENTY-SIX

What Closing Is All About

Closing Is a Process, Not an Event

Closing is the natural conclusion of the Bullet Selling process. It takes six steps, well executed, to open a relationship and close a sale. I call it natural because if you do a great job during the Pre-Call Planning, Building Rapport, Discovery, Tailored Solution, and Addressing Concerns steps, closing a sale is relatively easy. Still, nothing happens unless we get into the habit of asking for our buyer's business in an effective way. Few sales ever close without the sales professional first asking for the order.

The Psychology of Closing

Closing the sale makes many mere mortals tremble with apprehension. When you ask for the close, you have to face some of your demons eyeball-to-eyeball:

- Fear of rejection
- Fear of an empty pipeline
- Fear of success

Fear of rejection has to do with being afraid that buyers will tell you "no."

$500 Sales Tip!

You'll never regret the times you asked and were told "no." But you will regret when you didn't ask for the order because you were afraid.

—G.A. Bartick

Fear of an empty pipeline is another thing altogether. Having a full pipeline feels good no matter what, which is why I say full pipelines give many of us the illusion of success. Most poor performers have very full pipelines—I like to call them "clogged" pipelines because there is little movement in and out. Top performers tend to keep their pipelines lean and flowing, with potential new deals constantly flowing in and deals that are not going to close flowing out.

The fear of success is a little bit tricky for me because it deals with psychobabble, which I just don't understand. From what my brother Paul tells me, the fear of success can come from the belief that we are undeserving of all the rewards that come our way. The fear of success can also come from the fear of change. People get comfortable with their situation and avoid taking proactive measures to change, even if it means changing for the better. Either way, the fear of success breeds avoidance behavior and sabotages our success.

Closing Rewards the Persistent: A Lesson from Dr. Seuss

Being a sales professional is risky business and to become successful, you'll have to face rejection over and over and over again. That's why I think the best sales book ever written is *Green Eggs and Ham* by Dr. Seuss (aka Theodore Geisel). If you don't remember the storyline, it goes something like this:

Sam-I-Am is a sales professional. He is brimming with energy and enthusiasm and is trying to sell his buyer, a no-name skeptic, on the idea of trying green eggs and ham. At first the buyer rejects the proposal outright. Undeterred, Sam-I-Am asks for the order no fewer than 16 times. In

Did You Know...

Green Eggs and Ham is the fourth all-time best-selling hardcover children's book after:
1. *The Poky Little Puppy*
2. *The Tale of Peter Rabbit*
3. *Tootle*

Harry Potter and the Goblet of Fire comes in at #5. (I haven't heard of #1 and #3 either.)

the end Sam-I-Am's persistence pays off. He closes the sale and wins an appreciative buyer who says excitedly, "I do so like green eggs and ham! Thank you! Thank you, Sam-I-Am!"

From this best-selling children's book we learn three selling fundamentals:

1. Sam is selling a product, and although his buyer is not initially interested, Sam doesn't let that stop him from asking for the order.

2. Sam consistently offers the prospect a choice when trying to close the sale.

3. Sam refuses to give up. No matter how many times his buyer says "no," Sam keeps offering alternatives.

Now I am not suggesting that you pester your buyers, but most people give up too early in the sales process. We hear a no and retreat with our tails between our legs.

When-at-First-You-Don't-Succeed Success Stories

I am always intrigued by true stories of people who met with terrific resistance and persisted until they found sweet success. Here are a few of my favorites.

- When Alexander Graham Bell invented the telephone in 1876, it did not ring off the hook with calls from potential backers. After making a demonstration call, President Rutherford Hayes said, "That's an amazing invention, but who would ever want to use one of them?"

- Thomas Edison tried over 2,000 experiments before he got the lightbulb to work. He even tried a filament made of bamboo. A young reporter asked him how it felt to fail so many times. Edison said, "I never failed once. I invented the lightbulb. It just happened to be a 2,000-step process."

- In the 1940s another young inventor named Chester Carlson took his idea to 20 different corporations, including some of the biggest in the country. They all turned him down. In 1947, after seven long years of rejections, the Haloid Company, a tiny company in Rochester, New York, purchased the rights to his invention and process. The Haloid Company became the Xerox Corporation.

- In 1954 Jimmy Denny, manager of the Grand Ole Opry, fired a singer after one performance. He told him, "You ain't goin' nowhere, son. You ought to go back to drivin' a truck." Well, Elvis Presley paid him no mind. He went on to become the most popular singer in America.

- In 1962 four nervous young musicians played their first audition for the executives of the Decca recording company. The executives were not impressed. Turning down this group of musicians, one executive said, "We don't like their sound. Guitar groups are on the way out." The group was The Beatles.

I love these stories because they are about people who had to develop strong character to succeed. Character cannot be developed in peace and quiet. Only through struggle can the soul be strengthened, vision cleared, ambition inspired, and success achieved. A winner is not one who never fails, but one who never quits!

Blast from the Past!
Kites rise highest against the wind, not with it.

— Winston Churchill

CHAPTER TWENTY-SEVEN

Closing the Sale: Firming Up Details and Setting Expectations

Asking for the Order Is Closing

Closing is a process, but there is really only one part in the Bullet Selling process where we focus our energy on giving our buyers the opportunity to make a positive buying decision. Active closing really takes place in the Closing the Sale step. This chapter presents information that will increase your chances of closing the sale, but remember: Few sales ever close without asking for the order.

Asking for the Order Process

If you recall from the Tailored Solution step, the trial close is nothing more than a soft closing question. It's "soft" because it doesn't really ask for a hard yes or no, go or no go response. Instead, it asks for an opinion that indicates whether buyers are ready to move forward. We have asked trial close questions throughout the sales call to move the Bullet Selling process forward. But when we ask a trial close during the Closing the Sale step, we are *looking for a positive response* that we can follow with a hard close question that directly asks for a positive buying decision. After all, it's our jobs as sales professionals to help our buyers make these positive buying decisions.

There are two parts to asking for the order:

1. Trial close
2. Hard close (a call to action)

After we ask the trial close, we have to wait for buyers to give a positive response. If they give us a negative response, we have to revisit addressing concerns.

Here are some examples of trial close questions followed by a hard close:

Trial Close

In your opinion, does the way we've structured the delivery schedule work well for you? (wait for positive response)

Hard Close

So can we move forward and put in your first order then?

Trial Close

Are the terms and conditions of the proposal what you're looking for? (wait for positive response)

Hard Close

Great, then should I draw up the contract?

The What and the Why

We ask the trial close to gain a "yes" before asking for the order. This trial close generates a little momentum and increases buyers' receptivity. Therefore, it's important that we ask a trial close question that we know will generate a positive response. Once we get an initial "yes," we're ready to ask for the order.

Other Closing Techniques

I am not a fan of closing techniques other than the trial close and hard close. Our research shows that many buyers find closing techniques like the minor-point close or the assumptive close manipulative and sneaky.

☛ READY, AIM, FIRE!

Build Your Own Close

Now it's time to spend a few moments developing your own close. Think of two upcoming closing situations and for each one choose the closing question(s) you want to use.

Example

Company: The Phillips Restaurant Group

Closing Question(s): (trial close) So do you think the chefs in your restaurants will appreciate the freshness and quality of our meat, fish, and poultry products? (Wait for a "yes.") (hard close) Great, are you ready to move forward and make your first order?

Now it's your turn. Go ahead and write your responses on a separate sheet of paper, or use the template at www.silverbulletselling.com.

Practice Delivering Your Closing Questions

A lot is at stake when you ask your closing questions, so it's important to practice before delivering them.

1. Read your closing questions four to six times slowly until you begin to memorize them.
2. Practice saying your closing questions until you have them memorized and can communicate them without your notes.
3. Take a break.
4. Repeat steps 1 and 2 until your delivery is smooth and uncanned.
5. Using a tape recorder, record your delivery to hear what you sound like. Assess what you hear and adjust your delivery until you are very satisfied. Make sure your tone of voice is enthusiastic, not monotone.

Three Possible Outcomes

Once we've asked for the order, our buyers will give us one of three responses:

1. I want it
2. I want it but. . . .
3. I don't want it

Response #1: The "I Want It" Response—Taking Care of the Details and Setting Expectations

Congratulations! You've grabbed the brass ring and have made the sale. Now it's time for you to put the bow around it. A closing process called "summary of sale" will help you take care of the details (before they take care of you) and allow you to exceed your buyer's expectations. This is extremely important. We don't want one-time sales; we want buyers for life.

> ## Did you know...
>
> The brass ring became popular during the heyday of the carousel in the U.S. right around the turn of the 20th century. From this humble origin the "brass ring" has become synonymous with striving for the highest prize.

Here are the six issues we need to review with our buyers:

1. List the deliverables, including the product(s), service(s), feature(s), and option(s) the buyer has purchased.
2. List possible options the buyer chose not to purchase.
3. Go over the payment terms.
4. Identify communication preferences.
5. Review specific action items.
6. Summarize the agreement and the action steps with a written recap.

List the Deliverables

The selling process is a lot like courtship. To woo buyers, the sales professional makes promises and commitments. Because memory is so selective, the promises buyers think they heard might be different from the promises the sales professional thinks he made. And when buyers think they heard something you don't remember, you are going to lose. Period. After a sale is made, you just can't convince buyers that you did or didn't say something. That's why we review the deliverables by saying something like this:

Telecom Industry

Sales Professional:

> Kim, to make sure you and I are on the same page, I'm going to review all of the specific deliverables you're expecting from us. This will give you the opportunity to speak up if I've missed anything. How does that sound?

Buyer:

> Good idea.

Sales Professional:

> Terrific. We're taking an order for 75 new telephone wireless headsets model #CS50 because you wanted the longer roaming distance, along with 75 HL10 receiver lifters. They will be delivered to your law firm by June 7, attention Sherryl Bird. You also declined the extended warranty. The total investment including tax is $23,645.86. And that will be invoiced at net 30.

> I personally will be there the day the shipment arrives to ensure that all of the units arrive and, more importantly, to conduct a mini-training workshop for all of your associates so they'll be able to understand how the new headsets work.

> With that order each headset will come with an easy-to-use card-size guide that you can give to your associates, and we are throwing in an extra hundred guides for you to keep for the future. Does that cover everything we discussed in terms of deliverables, or did I leave anything out?

As you can see in this example, we go through the deliverables one by one to make sure we share the same understanding with our buyers. In some cases buyers will add additional deliverables or modify a deliverable, and that is fantastic news for you. It means you have just eliminated a future problem that might have hurt your relationship. The key here is the final question where you ask buyers to confirm that you have the deliverables right.

It is very important to take notes (mind mapping rides again!) and write down the deliverables as they were communicated in that brief exchange, especially if any were added or subtracted by the buyers. After the meeting, you'll recap this information to the buyers, and you'll need accurate notes so that your recap is on target. (We cover recaps later in Part 3.)

Go Over the Payment Terms

The next item to review is the financial terms of the agreement. Reviewing this item makes some sales professionals feel uncomfortable because they fear that a frank discussion about money might blow the deal. My experience with over 6,000 sales professionals tells me this is not true. In fact, your buyers want the financial terms to be clear because they want to know exactly how much they're paying and to eliminate billing problems before they arise. You'll be amazed at how many billing problems will disappear if you just review the payment terms at the point of sale.

Identify Communication Preferences

Another important topic that will certainly influence buyers' experiences is the way you communicate. Some buyers require a lot of communication, and some prefer less. Some like e-mail, some like in-person visits, and others like phone calls. However, you won't know for sure until you ask. Ideally, you'll find out exactly how much information your key contacts want and how they'd like it delivered. Here are some questions that could help you obtain this important information:

- *What is the best way to keep you informed in terms of progress: e-mail, phone calls, reports?*
- *How frequently would you like to hear from me?*
- *Ideally, what type of information would you like me to provide you with, and how often would you like to get it?*
- *If I did a spectacular job at keeping you informed, what would I ideally be doing?*

You need to understand, in the buyers' own words, what they want in terms of communication and then you need to repeat it back to them in the written recap.

Whenever possible, try to maintain one point of contact with buyers. It's much simpler and you avoid a lot of headaches. Communication begins to break down when too many people are involved.

Review Action Items

There may be additional commitments, deadlines, and action items that haven't been specifically spelled out by this point in the sales call. Closing is an opportunity to review those items. For instance, buyers may be expecting a phone call or a follow-up e-mail, or you might be expecting a signed contract faxed or mailed to your office. Make sure to take the time to discuss these items and ask buyers if there is anything else you need to do before you end the meeting. It is particularly important to include action items that the buyers are responsible for because, in many industries, their part of the deal will have a huge impact on your ability to execute. The three most important things to have on a list of action items are:

1. Action item defined
2. Who is accountable for the completion of that action item
3. Agreed-on deadline for that action item

A shorthand way of saying it is "who does what by when." You've probably guessed that you must write down all these commitments and review them with buyers in a written recap of the meeting. Here's what an action item table might look like for a new deal:

Who	Does What	By When
Adrienne	Fax a signed copy of the contract to G.A.'s office at 858-555-9210.	7/27
G.A. / Adrienne	Pre-call planning meeting to discuss roll-out	7/29
G.A.	G.A. on site in Seattle to conduct interviews	8/3

The Summary of Sale Checklist

Like the pre-call planning checklist, the summary of sale checklist makes sure none of the details falls through the cracks. It needs to be highly customized because different industries have very different closing details. I'm going to show you what my summary of sale checklist looks like, and then you can customize yours.

G.A.'s Summary of Sale Checklist

- ☐ Training and coaching programs selected
- ☐ Identify the different audiences to be trained/coached (# of participants)
- ☐ Dates of discovery
- ☐ Dates of development
- ☐ Identify client team to review materials
- ☐ Create material review timeline
- ☐ Date pilot begins
- ☐ Dates of delivery
- ☐ Financial terms
- ☐ Signed contract
- ☐ Key metrics identified
- ☐ Target metric goals
- ☐ Types and frequency of reports and communication of project information
- ☐ Communication preferences
- ☐ Written recap of closing meeting (and all meetings)

Before you create your own, brainstorm all the items that need to be on the list in no particular order. You can do that on a separate sheet of paper or go to silverbulletselling.com to download a free form.

Click Here!
You can print out your own Summary of Sale template by logging on to www.silverbulletselling.com.

Closing Requires a Well-Written Recap to Tie Up Loose Ends

The whole point of a well-written and quickly produced recap (preferably on the same business day, but certainly within 24 hours) is to help seal the deal even tighter while creating a unique and different experience for the buyer. The key here is to find a format and style that fits your business and industry, and to execute it quickly, consistently, and professionally. I like to keep my recaps short (one to three pages).

Most of your competitors aren't going to provide such a recap because it's "extra" work that doesn't have to get done. That's precisely where your competitive advantage kicks in. When you consistently do the things your competitors aren't willing to do, more buyers will want to do business with you. That's competitive difference in action, and that lays the groundwork for a successful relationship that will exceed buyers' expectations. This is the difference that will lock you in and lock your competition out. It's one thing to talk about your advantages, but it's another for buyers to experience them and ultimately brag about them. And when you can get your buyers bragging about you, your company, your service, and the overall buying experience, you are on your way to the highest level of sales success possible!

A Word about Exceeding Your Buyers' Expectations

Exceeding your buyers' expectations is at the heart of the Bullet Selling process because more often than not, it's a lot easier to sell more of your products and services to current buyers than it is to find new buyers.

The best way to achieve buyer loyalty and repeat business is to exceed buyers' expectations by underpromising and overdelivering. When you exceed your buyers' expectations, not only do they want to order more from you, but they also spread the good word. Happy buyers are a great source of referrals (more on that in Part 3). Also, in the business world, when buyers change jobs or companies they often take their best suppliers along with them.

Response #2: The "I Want It But" Response–Revisiting the Addressing Concerns Process

If a buyer says something like . . .

- "I'd like to run this by my boss and a few of my colleagues first . . ."
- "Let me get together with my people and make sure they don't have any questions . . ."
- "This sounds good but let me check with my wife . . ."

. . . then we know he isn't completely in and we should dip back into the addressing concerns process. At the very least make sure you agree on a date your buyer will get back to you.

Response #3: The "I Don't Want It" Response–Handle Their Concerns or Walk Away?

When I get buyers who are not ready to buy, I have a decision to make. Should I put more time and effort into handling their concerns, or should I shake hands and walk away? It really all depends on what their reasoning is. Sometimes it has to do with timing and a buyer asks me to wait to move forward. That decision is easy. I ask these buyers if I can keep in touch during the interim and then I make sure to keep them in my pipeline.

However, when other reasons are prohibiting buyers from moving forward, I have to make a decision on a case-by-case basis. Recognize that the time you spend with indecisive buyers is time taken away from good, definite buyers who put sales on your scoreboard and commissions into your pocket.

Tips on Closing

1. If you don't A-S-K, then you don't G-E-T. No sale ever happened without asking for the order.

2. Remember that closing is really the process of opening a relationship.

3. Closing really happens throughout the Bullet Selling process.

4. Buyers often make their buying decisions based on how you handle their concerns. Focus your attention on helping buyers by sincerely addressing their concerns.

5. Do not overpromise just to get a positive buying decision. You set yourself up for future disappointments and decreased repeat business.

6. Write down every promise/commitment you make so that you can overdeliver.

7. Summarize the details of every agreement and sale. Buyers often forget or think they heard something you didn't commit to. Clear this up by summarizing.

8. Manage buyers' expectations carefully. Ask them what they expect in terms of follow-up. Write it down and send it back to your buyers in a recap with your promise to fulfill those expectations.

9. Tell your buyers up front about any expectations you cannot fulfill. It is better to proactively prevent misunderstandings than to work it out later after the damage is done.

10. Make sure you communicate to your buyers as you complete the action items assigned to you.

PART THREE

AUXILIARY FIREPOWER

CHAPTER TWENTY-EIGHT

Additional Ammunition

The Bullet Selling process even helps me address con-cerns from my wife. And that's a beautiful thing!

—G.A. Bartick

Okay, you've been introduced to the six steps of the Bullet Selling process and have learned how to close more sales by creating a unique and different buying experience. This was the easy part. The next challenge is putting in the work to become effective at executing the process. In Chapter 3 I told you this wasn't going to be easy; if it was, everyone would do it and they wouldn't pay us as much. The work ahead is for you to continuously revise and practice all of the different components of the process:

- Pre-call planning
- Agenda statement
- Credibility statement
- Discovery questions
- Discovery summary
- Business philosophy
- Presenting tailored solutions
- Addressing concerns process
- Vaccinating against the competition

- Asking for the order
- Closing the sale

Reserve Power

We have neatly laid out the steps of the process but, as we all know, it just doesn't happen like that in real life. The sales interaction is a living, breathing thing and since buyers do not know the steps of the process, they do not always follow it exactly. For this reason one of the goals of this book is to fill you with Reserve Power—the ability to have appropriate responses at the ready you can customize for any specific situation. For instance, if someone were to ask you "What is your company's competitive advantage?" you could go right into your business philosophy. Or if someone at a dinner party asked, "What do you do?" you could respond with your entire 90-second credibility statement. Someone can say, "Tell me a little bit about your company," and you could go right into features, bridges, and benefits.

Reserve Power is all about having bullets in your chamber. The Bullet Selling process gives you all kinds of bullets to use in all sorts of situations. Having a full arsenal of information and processes at the ready for deployment in any situation is what Reserve Power is all about.

More Bullets for Your Chamber

The additional components of the Bullet Selling process that we'll learn about here can help you in different business situations and at home in your personal life. They include:

- Meeting recaps
  Use these whenever you want to make sure you are both on the same page.
- Generating referrals
  Use this component when you want to ask your buyers to refer business to you.

- The conversation stack
    Use this when you are networking at a company function or at a holiday cocktail party.
- Time management techniques
    Use these techniques whenever you want to accomplish more in less time.

Meeting Recaps

For me a meeting isn't adjourned until the meeting recap is e-mailed to my buyers. I can't begin to tell you the kind of value I get out of the 30 minutes it takes me to write and send out a meeting recap. It's a very important part of my business acumen. First of all, it takes buyers by surprise. It is usually the first deliverable my buyers get from me, and immediately I am exceeding their expectations by generating that unique and different buying experience from the get-go. Second, the meeting recap includes all of the action items that need to be completed and my buyers and I use it to keep our project moving forward. Third, the recap summarizes all of the important decisions that were discussed and my buyers like to keep them as a written record. Finally, the recap ensures that my buyers and I understand each other. If something is incorrect on the meeting recap, we can discuss it before anyone makes a costly mistake.

What Goes into a Meeting Recap?

A recap documents all of the important information discussed during a face-to-face or telephone meeting. The recap should include these elements:

- Purpose of the meeting
    I just cut and paste this from the printed agenda I prepared for the meeting during my pre-call planning.
- Participants
    Who participated in the meeting.

- Agenda items

     The topics that were discussed and the highlights of the discussion. Under each agenda item I fill in what we discussed during the meeting.

- Decisions made

     This section documents any decisions that were made.

- Action items

     This is the same three-column grid that we introduced in Chapter 27 that includes who does what by when.

Here's a recap from a meeting my brother and I had with Barry Davidson and Company, a regional brokerage house in California.

Telephone Meeting Recap
July 16, 2008

Purpose:

To discuss the details of the recruiting course for Managers and the compensation program for new hires

Attendees:

Barry Davidson

- Tim Bowen
- Susan Morris

OutSell

- Paul Bartick
- G.A. Bartick

Topics Covered:

Review of Recruiting Course

- Tim and Susan have reviewed the course and approve the content with the following additions:

    1. For transfers we are targeting mid-level producers in the $500,000 range.

2. The Orange County office will screen and qualify potential transfers via phone and pass qualified and interested candidates on to the Managers in their branches.

3. Managers will continue to conduct in-person interviews.

- The firm is also going to be working with a professional recruiter in San Francisco. Tim to confirm name of recruiter.

  1. The recruiter will pre-screen transfer candidates and pass on qualified and interested candidates to the Branch Manager.

  2. Dennis has worked with the recommended recruiter.

- Barry Davidson is going to focus more on internet postings and less on print ads.

- Eight-hour course scheduled for July 26th. All managers will be trained at the Beverly Hills office training room.

Review of Compensation Plan

- Tim and Susan reviewed the draft compensation plans for rookies and new hires and feel they are getting close.

- The firm is looking to adjust its payout grid to continue to be competitive in the market. In doing so, the firm wants to introduce deferred payments into the formula.

- Tim prefers a grid that provides stepping-stone incentives starting from a small production of $100,000 to motivate and reward success.

- Objective here is to recruit, train and retain advisors. Tim would be satisfied with a 40% retention rate from hire to grid.

Action Items:

Who	Does What	By When
Tim	Confirm the name of the San Francisco recruiter and notify Paul via e-mail	July 18 COB
Paul	Revise content of recruiting course and submit to Tim and Susan for sign off	July 18 COB
Tim and Susan	Sign off on content	July 21 COB
Paul	Send printed materials including manual and job aids to printer	July 23 OOB
G.A.	Deliver Recruiting Workshop	July 25

This recap was delivered to Tim and Susan via e-mail on the afternoon of July 16, three hours after the meeting ended. The next morning Paul and I received a short e-mail from the President thanking us for our good work. The meeting recap shows buyers what great service is.

Generating Referrals

According to BNET, the popular online resource for business executives, a referral is 15 times more likely to do business with you than a cold prospect. With odds like that, it's no wonder top-performing sales professionals commit much of their energy to asking for, contacting, and following up on referrals. Would you rather make another 100 cold calls or make 5 to clients and effectively ask them for referrals? The choice is yours.

The way we ask for referrals will have a huge impact on the number and the quality of the referrals we get. Most sales professionals ask for referrals in this way:

Poor Example

Sales Professional:
> Hello, Sandy. This is G.A. It's been great working with you and I was wondering if you know of any people you could refer me to that might want to use my services.

Buyer:
> I'd love to help you out, G.A. You've been great. But I can't think of anyone off the top of my head. Why don't I think about it. Give me a call in a couple of days.

Sales Professional:
> That's sounds great. How about if I give you a call on Wednesday afternoon.

So Wednesday rolls around and I give Sandy a call. Here's how the conversation typically goes:

Poor Example (Cont'd)

Sales Professional:
> Hello, Sandy, G.A. here. I was just wondering if you had a chance to think about any referrals you could send my way.

Buyer:
> Hey, G.A. I've been so busy, I'm sorry. How about I think about it over the weekend and you give me a call early next week?

The weekend passes and I decide to give Sandy an extra day to think about it. On Tuesday morning my tickler system tells me to give Sandy a call.

Poor Example (Cont'd)

Sales Professional:
  Hello, this is G.A. for Sandy, please.

Gatekeeper:
  May I ask her what this is in reference to?

Sales Professional:
  Yes, I'm following up with a conversation we had last week.

Gatekeeper:
  Can you hold while I check to see if she's in? What was your name again?

Sales Professional:
  It's G.A. G period, A period.

Gatekeeper (a few moments later . . .)
  I'm sorry A.G. [they're always mixing it up], *Sandy is in a meeting right now. May I connect you to her voice mail?*

Now Sandy's not taking my call because she feels bad for not coming through with a referral. And all of a sudden my great relationship with her is a little strained. Needless to say, this isn't a very effective way to ask for referrals.

People have a mental Rolodex in their heads. When we ask, "Who do you know . . ." they have to cull through the thousands of names they know. All we want is one or two so we have to help them narrow it down.

Ideally, we want the person we are requesting the referral from to think of people who would be interested in working with or buying from someone like us. From our research we have created a four-step generating referrals process.

Step 1. Thank the buyer for their business

Step 2. Describe your ideal referral

Step 3. Point out places where the buyer may interact with the ideal referral

Step 4. Ask for an introduction

Here's the generating referrals process in action:

Financial Services Industry

Step 1. Thank Buyer for Their Business

> *Nancy, I want to thank you for allowing me to service you over the past two years. I really value your trust and will do everything I can to keep earning your business.*

Step 2. Describe Your Ideal Referral

> *As you probably know, I make my living by helping clients reach their long-term financial goals. I mostly work with C-level officers, small business owners, and even attorneys and CPAs.*

Step 3. Point Out Places Where Clients May Interact with the Ideal Referral

> *You may know some of these people from your association with the YMCA. You might want to refer a neighbor of yours or a friend from your tennis club.*

Step 4. Ask for an Introduction

> *Is there anyone who comes to mind that you could introduce me to who might be interested in the benefits of investing with me and building a better financial future?*

☞ READY, AIM, FIRE!

Build Your Own Referral Interaction

Think of a buyer you want to ask for a referral and use the steps that follow to build your own referral interaction. Go ahead and write your answers on a separate sheet of paper or download the forms at www.silverbulletselling.com.

Step 1. Thank the buyer for his business

Step 2. Describe your ideal referral

Step 3. Point out places where the buyer may interact with the ideal referral

Step 4. Ask for an introduction

Practice Delivering Your Own Referral Interaction

It's time to practice the referral interaction you just developed.

1. Stand up with your customized referral interaction in hand.

2. Read your referral interaction aloud twice verbatim, including the steps of the process.

3. Read your referral interaction four to six times slowly until you begin to memorize the process (not the words, but the steps of the process).

4. Practice saying your referral interaction until you have the process memorized and can communicate it without your notes.

5. Take a break.

6. Repeat steps 3 and 4 until your delivery is smooth and uncanned.

7. Using a tape recorder, record your delivery to hear what you sound like. Assess what you hear and adjust your delivery until you are very satisfied. Make sure your tone of voice is enthusiastic, not monotone.

Working the Room: Building Rapport in Casual Conversation

What happens when your buyer introduces you to the President of his company at a holiday party? What do you talk about? The weather? You need more ammunition in your arsenal than that. That's why we use a nifty tool called the conversation stack.

The conversation stack is useful in casual settings such as cocktail parties and other social gatherings. It's a great technique for carrying on a meaningful conversation with a complete stranger and building positive rapport while doing it. The conversation stack is a logical questioning flow that will uncover much of what is important to the person you're speaking with and allowing you to make contact on a more personal level. It will help you connect with that company President and make a positive first impression.

The Conversation Stack

What is a stack? A stack is a memory device that you can use to remember a list of items. It can be as short as 3 to 4 items, and with practice you can extend it to 15, maybe 20 items. This stack has 7 items. Try this:

Clear your mind and be ready to visualize objects as I describe them to you. The more ridiculous the items in the stack, the easier it is to remember.

Picture this in your mind:

1. First, think of a huge six-foot brass NAMEPLATE.
2. Perched atop the nameplate is a HOUSE with a purple door.
3. Next, you see a bunch of KIDS throwing water balloons out of the windows of the house.
4. Out of the chimney of the house you see a gigantic WORK GLOVE reaching up into the sky.
5. This work glove then grabs hold of an AIRPLANE as it flies by.
6. Then you look inside the airplane and you see that every one of the passengers is wearing SKIS.
7. And on the end of the skis there are LIGHTBULBS.

Right now many of you are probably thinking, "What is G.A. talking about?" Before you're completely convinced that I've lost it, let me explain how this works. In your mind do you see the seven items of the stack?

1. Nameplate
2. House

3. Kids

4. Work glove

5. Airplane

6. Skis

7. Lightbulb

Just like that, you are now equipped to carry on a meaningful conversation with anyone anywhere (provided you speak the same language).

What Does All of This Mean?

These seven objects are memory joggers of topics you can discuss with your new best friend. I'll show you what each symbol represents, along with a few questions you can use. Once you ask the first question, ask clarifying questions to learn more.

Conversation Stack

1. Nameplate: **Your name**
Pronunciation
Spelling
Heritage *(e.g., family origin, ethnic background)*

2. House: **Where you live**
Where do you live?
How long have you lived there?
How did you come to live there?
What do you like most about where you live?
Where are you originally from?

3. Kids: **Family life**
Do you have any kids?
Are they teenagers, or younger?
What do they like to do?
Where do they go to school?

4. Work Glove: **Work**
What do you do for a living?
How long have you been doing it?
Where did you work before?
How did you get into the field?
What do you like best about your work?
What do you find most challenging?

5. Airplane: **Travel**
Do you travel for pleasure?
Do you travel for business?
Where do you like to go?
Where was your last trip?
Do you have any trips planned?

6. Skis: **Hobbies and fun**
What do you like to do for fun?
Do you have any hobbies?
Do you ... *(e.g., golf, ski, run, bike, etc.)*

7. Lightbulb: **Topics of personal interest**
What do you think of...?
(e.g., health of the economy, news of the day)

*(Do not debate if you disagree. The goal here is to
find something in common you can discuss together.)*

Using the Conversation Stack

Go through the topics of the conversation stack until you find a common area of interest that you can spend some time on. If your conversation stalls on one topic, then go on to the next. The key here is to find common ground and carry on a conversation. I've engaged people for over an hour using this stack and sometimes I don't even get past Topic 5 (travel).

The Conversation Stack at Work

I have run many workshops and classes and have introduced the conversation stack to many companies. During class I have participants stand up with their colleagues and walk through the conversation stack for two minutes. Often people learn more about a colleague during that exercise than they have learned working next to them for several years. Once during the exercise, two colleagues who worked two offices down from each other for seven years realized they were from the same city, had gone to competing high schools, and were second cousins!

 Click Here!
If you want to hear the conversation stack in action,
log on to www.silverbulletselling.com.

Time Management Techniques

Sales professionals always have too much to do. Cold calls, pre-call planning, sales calls, team meetings, follow-up, recaps, e-mail, voice mail, and the list just goes on. It only makes sense that a big part of your success depends on how much you can get done each day. Every one of us is given 10,080 minutes each week, and how much we get done depends on our ability to manage our time.

Good time management is much more than just being organized. It's really about building a time management system to ensure deadlines are met, promises are kept, and work is consistently completed when our buyers (and managers) expect it to be done.

The best time management system I've come across is David Allen's Getting Things Done process. I am a huge fan of David Allen. I've read his book, purchased his CDs, been to his seminar twice, and taught the executives I coach many of his key fundamentals. Check it out.

Time Management Self-Analysis

Complete the following questionnaire to analyze how well you manage your time and to discover your areas of opportunity.

Circle the number that best describes your situation.

1 = Rarely	3 = Usually
2 = Occasionally	4 = Always

1	2	3	4	I begin each day with an organized master to-do list that includes all time-sensitive activities.
1	2	3	4	When I make a commitment to a buyer or manager to call them or complete a task by a given date, that task goes into my time-management system.
1	2	3	4	My calendar system is effective enough to track all of the tasks I need to accomplish on any given day/week/month.
1	2	3	4	I can find the names, phone numbers, addresses, and information I need quickly and easily.
1	2	3	4	I can look back on any given day and track what I accomplished and what tasks I completed.
1	2	3	4	I work a consistent schedule each day so my day is reasonably predictable.
1	2	3	4	Information and files on my desk are well organized and are easy to find.
1	2	3	4	I know the deadlines I have to meet each week, and prioritize my time so that they are met.
1	2	3	4	I spend at least 15 minutes each day planning.
1	2	3	4	Before I make a phone call, I carefully plan to make sure I cover as many issues as I can to avoid needing to call back again.
1	2	3	4	I take good notes on phone calls and document them.

Scoring your test: Add up your score _____

11-22	Your time management approach is significantly reducing your performance.
23-34	Your time management approach is inconsistent. Some days it works for you, and on others it works against you.
35-44	You are consistent in the way you manage your time. You are practicing time-tested techniques to produce predictable results.

Time Management Skills

Here are some key techniques that will help you manage your time more effectively.

Time Blocking

Time blocking is the practice of breaking your day into blocks of time. It's a great way to bring order to your day. For example, from 7:45 to 8:00 I do nothing but plan my day. Then, from 8:00 to 8:30, I do nothing but answer my e-mails and return phone calls. This means that I don't review the files that just came in or write the call recap from yesterday. Time blocking requires discipline and is very effective for very busy people.

A Day in the Life of G.A. *Bartick*

7:45 A.M.–8:00 A.M.

- Plan my day

8:00 A.M.–8:30 A.M.

- Answer e-mails
- Return phone calls

8:30 A.M.–9:00 A.M.

- Check in with OutSell project managers
- Check e-mail and voice mail at 10 minutes to the hour

9:00 A.M.–10:00 A.M.

- Client work
- Check email and voice mail at 10 minutes to the hour

10:00 A.M.–10:15 A.M.

- Take a walk

10:15 A.M.–12:00 P.M.

- Client work

- Check e-mail and voice mail at 10 minutes to the hour

12:00 P.M.–1:00 P.M.

- Lunch

1:00 P.M.–1:30 P.M.

- Sort mail and respond
- Give checks to Chris to remote deposit

1:30 P.M.–2:30 P.M.

- Answer e-mails
- Return phone calls

2:30 P.M.–3:30 P.M.

- Client work
- Check e-mail and voice mail at 10 minutes to the hour

3:30 P.M.–3:45 P.M.

- Take a walk

3:45 P.M.–5:30 P.M.

- Client work
- Check e-mail and voice mail at 10 minutes to the hour

5:30 P.M.–6:00 P.M.

- Plan for tomorrow. Iron briefcase
- Review "To Do/To Call" list
- Go home and enjoy a relaxing, fun-filled evening with the family

Go ahead and create your own time blocks on a separate page or use the template at www.silverbulletselling.com.

Batching Like Tasks

When we batch like tasks together, we generally save time. If you have any repetitive activities, such as adding contacts to your Customer Relationship Management (CRM) tool, getting marketing material ready to be mailed, or returning phone calls, you are most efficient when you can complete them at the same time. I may wait until I have three or four phone calls and then make them all right in a row. I seem to get in a rhythm and become more effective and efficient as I go.

Predictable Time

In a high-activity environment with lots of buyer contact, a predictable schedule is very helpful. For instance, you may inform your team members that every day, without exception, you will be calling in orders from 5:30 to 6:00. You then ask them not to call you during that time unless it is an emergency. This way you can stay focused and on task without interruption.

All-in-One Calls

In a high-touch sales environment, you must make a variety of calls to buyers. Taking a little extra time (i.e., pre-call plan) before each call to brainstorm all the possible agenda items you could cover can dramatically reduce the number of calls you have to make and the amount of time it takes for buyers to follow through.

When I was a mortgage banker, I would open a buyer's file and realize I needed to call to get a copy of his most recent paycheck. I would make the call and ask my buyer to fax it. Then, just after I hung up, I would realize that I also needed a copy of his 401(k) statement. So I would call again and apologize before I asked for the statement. Then, after digging a little deeper into the file, I'd realize that I needed to get one more month of bank statements from him. This time, when the buyer answered the phone, he didn't even say "Hello." Instead, he impatiently blurted, "What do you need this time, G.A.?"

I could have avoided annoying my buyer if I had spent a few minutes pre-call planning and looking for all the things I could take care of in one call.

Organized Contact Information

Several time management studies have shown that a significant amount of time is wasted looking up information like phone numbers and addresses. Top performers have a system (usually electronic) that quickly files names and numbers so they can be accessed efficiently.

Do the Worst First

Doing the worst first is actually a stress-reducing fundamental, but it is also a tremendous time saver. At the beginning of each day identify the most unpleasant activities you don't want to do. Instead of putting them off, do them first and get them out of the way. Once they're done, you'll feel better and nothing will be hanging over your head.

I have a tendency to procrastinate just a little. This is especially true with something I don't want to do. As a sales manager, sometimes I must have uncomfortable conversations with poor performers. I'll come in at the start of the day with every intention of getting the conversation done with by 9:30. At 9:00 I'll look out and see the sales professional on the phone, so I'll put it off. A couple of hours later I'll decide that I should do the deed, but I'll find some other rationalization and I wait some more.

I'll put it off until I finally have no choice, but you know what the strange thing is? After spending hours and sometimes days dreading doing something, the outcome is never nearly as bad as I had made it out to be in my mind. Get 'er done!

What's Next?

Consider this your formal introduction into the world of the Bullet Selling process. This may be the closing chapter of this book, but it is really the opening chapter of your journey to becoming a Bullet Selling sharpshooter.

Practice all of the tools and techniques we've discussed in this book. To become good at this stuff, you have to use it every day.

And of course, be patient. Don't expect to be an expert at the process right away. It will take you about a month of constant practice until you start to feel comfortable. If you're in a short sales cycle, by the time you're in your second month of practice, you will start to close more sales and see positive results. It will take slightly longer if you're in a business with a long sales cycle.

The Silver Bullet Community

You're not alone out there. The Silver Bullet community has over 20,000 members and is growing all the time. The "clubhouse" can be found online at www.silverbulletselling.com. There you'll find everything we have to offer including templates, worksheets, articles, white papers, Bullet Selling products, and a blog where our members communicate with each other.

I am constantly on the road giving seminars across the United States about different pieces of the Bullet Selling process. To see when I will be in your city, go to the web site and check my schedule.

The Bullet Selling process changed my life. It has allowed me to realize my dreams (desired situation), and I am committed to spreading the word so that others can do the same. We would love to hear from you. If you have a success story, useful strategies, inspirational stories, questions, comments, concerns, or even a compliment, we want to hear from you. E-mail me directly at ga@silverbulletselling.com or call me at 858-759-5306. I look forward to hearing from you. See you on the road!

OutSell Consulting: "Our Business Is Your Business"™

OutSell Consulting specializes in improving the performance of sales and customer service organizations. We do this by helping sales professionals and customer service reps communicate more effectively to create a world-class buying experience for their buyers.

OutSell Driving Principles

OutSell is committed to four principles:

1. Excellence
2. Passion
3. Collaboration
4. Integrity

Four Spokes of OutSell

OutSell Consulting is comprised of four different businesses:

1. OutSell Consulting

     This is our consulting business where we work with sales and customer service teams.

2. OutSell Call Center

     OutSell runs its own call center outsourcing operation where our team creates a world-class buyer experience for our clients.

3. OutSell Direct Sales Team

     OutSell has its own direct sales team which sells our clients' products directly to businesses and consumers.

4. Bullet Selling Seminars

     OutSell delivers the Bullet Selling process to the general public through seminars on topics such as sales, coaching and management, customer service, time management, and creating success on purpose.

OutSell Consulting offers these services:

- Sales training and consulting
- Customer service training and consulting
- Executive coaching
- Sales management training and consulting
- Call center management and outsourcing
- Direct sales training, consulting, and outsourcing
- Presentation skills training
- Train the trainer
- Keynote speeches for conventions and sales meetings

For more information on OutSell Consulting and our products and services, feel free to visit our web sites for contact information:

www.outsellconsulting.com

www.silverbulletselling.com

Index